SOLIHULL SIXTH FORM COLLEGE
THE LEARNING CENTRE

CHECKED   JUL 2008

D0487915

# GOING DOWN

# Going Down
## Football In Crisis
### How the game went from boom to bust

## Simon Banks

MAINSTREAM
PUBLISHING

EDINBURGH AND LONDON

Rec  2 4 NOV 2003
Stock no.  2 1 9 2 5
Class
796
·334
BAN

Labels G
T ✓

Copyright © Simon Banks, 2002
All rights reserved
The moral right of the author has been asserted

First published in Great Britain in 2002 by
MAINSTREAM PUBLISHING (EDINBURGH) LTD
7 Albany Street
Edinburgh EH1 3UG

ISBN 1 84018 637 2

No part of this book may be reproduced or transmitted in any form or by any
other means without the permission in writing from the publisher, except by a
reviewer who wishes to quote brief passages in connection with a review
written for insertion in a magazine, newspaper or broadcast.

Copyright permissions cleared by the author. The author has tried to trace all
copyright details but where this has not been possible and amendments are
required, the publisher will be pleased to make any necessary arrangements at
the earliest opportunity.

A catalogue record for this book is available from the British Library

Typeset in Berkeley and Gill Condensed

Printed in Great Britain by
Creative Print and Design Wales

# Contents

# Acknowledgements

This book is the result of the last four years I have spent as a journalist covering the business of football. During that time I have been surprised at the willingness of those involved in running the game at the highest level to discuss candidly their views and opinions of the game. It is not possible to mention here all the people who have helped me produce this book. Many of them did not even know they were doing so and nor did I until Mainstream Publishing commissioned a book on football's financial crisis in March 2002.

Two club chairmen were particularly helpful in granting me interviews as part of the research for this book. Peter Ridsdale of Leeds United and David Sheepshanks of Ipswich Town are quite rare among club chairmen in that they consistently look beyond the narrow interests of their own clubs and take a wider view of the game in general. That their contributions are not quoted at length in this book is due to the reticence of some of their counterparts whose contributions would have provided a wider range of opinions. That said, Ridsdale and Sheepshanks' contributions were crucial to the book and I thank them for their time.

Over the last four years several other senior executives at various clubs have been more than willing to assist me in trying to understand the business of football and were always willing to provide information and opinions. I would particularly like to thank Steve Kind at Leicester City, Steve Stride and Mark Ansell at Aston Villa and Geoffrey Richmond at Bradford City for their assistance over the years.

Football business journalism is a specialised field and few journalists are fortunate enough to be able to cover it exclusively, but those who do are remarkably supportive of others who work in the field. David Conn, author of the seminal *The Football Business*, has not only been extremely helpful over the years, but actively encouraged me to write this book, for which I am very grateful. Alex Fynn, author of numerous entertaining and knowledgeable titles on the subject was also very helpful, particularly on the subject of the formation of the Premier League in which he was personally involved. I have worked on several stories with the *News of the World*'s Geoff Sweet and he has been constantly supportive and has become a good friend. Thanks also go to Matthew Glendinning of *Sport Business*, the *Guardian*'s Vivek Chaudhary and the *London Evening Standard*'s David Bond.

There are a lot of numbers in this book and most of them have been supplied by Deloitte & Touche Sport, headed by Gerry Boon. Deloitte's *Annual Review of Football Finance* has proved indispensable in writing this book and Alex Phillips in particular has been more than willing to provide copious information at short notice. I am sure that he will prove to be a great success in his new post with UEFA's Professional Football and Competitions Department in Nyon and I wish him all the best.

Others who have provided me with the data and information that has been essential in compiling this book include *Soccer Investor* editor Oliver Butler, *Guardian* archivist Mike Pike and *Sport Business*'s Johno Fullerton and I thank them for their help.

Anthony King from the University of Exeter was particularly helpful with Chapter 6 and his latest book about European football is eagerly anticipated. Patrick Murphy at the University of Leicester was most helpful in assisting me with the research for Chapter 3 and it is hoped that the *Singer & Friedlander Football Review* finds a new sponsor soon.

Angela Breckenridge worked tirelessly in editing the manuscript prior to its submission for publication and her suggestions as to how it could be improved were gratefully received. If this book is readable it is largely because of her expert advice.

I would also like to thank the editorial team at Mainstream for their patience and understanding and Bill Campbell for commissioning the book, as well as my agent John Ireland.

Finally, the greatest thanks must go to my wife Shirley, who has been so supportive during the research and writing of this book. It is by no means an exaggeration to say that without her love and support this book would not have been written.

# Introduction

ENGLISH FOOTBALL IS IN CRISIS. UP TO 30 ENGLISH CLUBS ARE FACING BANKRUPTCY AND hundreds of players are heading towards the dole queue. Yet football's financial crisis comes at a time when the game is as popular as it has ever been and more money than ever before is coming into the game. Top players are earning millions while clubs have become multi-million-pound businesses, in some cases quoted on the stock exchange. In 2000, English football signed television deals worth over £2bn and the Premier League could justifiably claim to be the richest league in the world, turning over more than £1bn a year. Two years later and the game is in crisis and facing a very uncertain future.

There are those who claim that football is not in crisis, merely experiencing a cyclical dip in its financial fortunes. Ipswich Town Chairman David Sheepshanks prefers the term 'recession' which suggests that there will be a recovery. Indeed, the history of football has seen years of growth and then decline. Following the end of the Second World War until the early 1950s, football, in common with several sports, experienced a massive increase in public interest and attendances at matches. Attendances dropped throughout the mid '50s to the early '60s and started to increase again after England's World Cup victory in 1966. By the end of the 1970s attendances declined again until the end of the 1980s when the trend was once again reversed. Since the formation of the Premier League and the implementation of the Taylor Report, which required all stadia in the top two divisions to become all-seater and consequently depressed gates, attendances have risen again and year on year the Premier League and Football League attendances continue to rise. It is clear then that public interest is as high, if not higher, than ever before, yet clubs are on the verge of bankruptcy and as many as 800 players are facing the dole. At the top of the English game, there is a certain amount of complacency about the current crisis. Unveiling yet another increase in profits in March 2002, as ITV Digital was crashing towards liquidation and seeking to renegotiate its TV deal with the Football League, Manchester United's Chief Executive Peter Kenyon said:

> The key message here is that the Premier League is still delivering audiences and ultimately audiences are what will secure advertising, and that's why we believe you've got to look at the Premier League deal as a different product to that of the Football League.[1]

While Kenyon may be right in that Manchester United do not have to worry too much about the crisis in the Football League, other Premier League clubs cannot afford to be as complacent; only 8 of the 22 clubs that started as inaugural members of the Premier League in 1992 have remained as continuous members.

The Football League's ill-fated television deal with the bankrupt platform ITV Digital is the most high-profile manifestation of the current crisis, but the crisis is not confined to the Football League, or even English football. Top English clubs are struggling to compete in Europe against the backdrop of an overcrowded domestic fixture list and the demands of international football on their multinational squads, leading them to field weakened teams in cup competitions. In Italy clubs are struggling under mounting debts, and failing to dominate European club competitions as they have done in the past. In Germany the Bundesliga has had to seek government help after the collapse of the Kirch media empire left the professional game with a £120m shortfall. Even the World Cup, the most popular sporting event in the world, has not escaped the threat of financial meltdown with the collapse of Kirch and FIFA's marketing partner ISL putting the financial future of FIFA, the tournament's owners, in jeopardy. Meanwhile, a time bomb is ticking away beneath the surface of the English game: the massive levels of debt that clubs have accumulated as they attempt to break into Europe, stay in the Premier League or just get into it. When that bomb eventually goes off, there will be high-profile casualties.

In order to understand how football's bubble came to burst it must first be established how it became inflated in the first place. The formation of the Premier League ten years ago provided the context within which the football boom took place and will therefore feature prominently in this book. When the Premier League was unveiled it received the backing of the Football Association because it was promoted as being for the good of all football, from the grass-roots to the England team. In Chapter 3 I examine whether the Premiership has succeeded in this aim and ask if it should continue to receive the FA's unconditional support.

The rise in the importance of television to football is a relatively recent phenomenon, predated by a realisation by television of football's importance to the medium. Even as late as the 1980s many clubs were opposed to live-coverage matches, but now most clubs, along with the governing bodies, see the game as just yet more television programming, with the needs of television now seen as more important than those of the paying spectator. Now that the value of TV rights is set to fall, will clubs and leagues set up and run their own TV channels? Or will football return to the old days when only the FA Cup final was televised? In Chapter 6 I examine the ever-changing relationship between football and television. There is a trend towards clubs, particularly the large ones, wanting more control over their own TV rights and one of the consequences of this trend could be the end of the Premier League, as its main purpose has been to collectively sell its member clubs' TV rights. If it no longer has that role then its member clubs may justifiably ask: 'What is the point of the Premier League?'

When looking at the state of English football, the question that keeps arising is 'Who runs football?': the clubs, the FA or the television companies? The answer is that all have some control, but nobody is either willing or able to take full responsibility for the game's direction. Another common question is 'Who owns football?'. The 1990s saw massive investment in the game, from merchant banks to venture capitalists, sponsors to TV companies, as well as a number of wealthy individuals. But what about the supporters, who for years have financed the game through paying at the gate and more recently by subscribing to pay-TV? Do they not deserve a say in how the game is run? When clubs go bust it is the supporters who are left to try and pick up the pieces. When a club is thriving they are often treated with little more than thinly veiled contempt.

The late 1990s saw clubs rush to the stock market in a 'dash for cash' which made some chairmen very rich. Most shareholders, however, have had their fingers burnt and seen the value of their investments decline considerably. Now several clubs are considering following Nottingham Forest and going back into private ownership. Who owns football is a question that I will attempt to address in Chapter 2 and in the concluding chapter, but suffice to say that the rise of the supporters' trust movement, under the auspices of the government-funded Supporters Direct, suggests that a new ownership model may be emerging.

Without doubt the major beneficiaries of the football boom have been the players, whose wages have increased exponentially. In addition to enjoying riches beyond the dreams of players from previous generations, thanks to the Bosman ruling today's players are also protected by European labour law and are free to walk out on clubs for the most spurious of reasons. How will the players and their representatives respond to a sharp decline in their incomes? The players' union has been at the forefront of bailing out ailing clubs and recently threatened to strike in order to obtain a share of television money, but are not the players themselves, along with their agents and their union, the PFA, at least partly responsible for football's crisis by demanding more and more of the increasing money coming into the game? If so, they must surely shoulder some responsibility for taking the game out of crisis.

After the 1999 cash for votes scandal the Football Association attempted to re-brand itself as the caring face of football governance, with a new management structure, new headquarters and a new chief executive, but still it continues to score own goal after own goal. From the failed bid to host the 2006 World Cup finals to the fiasco that is the Wembley Stadium saga, the FA has shown itself to be at best incompetent and at worst negligent. The Football League has seen itself increasingly marginalised since the formation of the Premiership and with the recent crisis over television rights, questions are being asked as to whether the League has any kind of future. The recent signing of a £95m four-year television deal with Sky by the Football League has been portrayed as saving the Football League from financial oblivion, not least by the Rupert Murdoch-owned press, but some League chairmen are questioning the judgement of the League's executive and chairman in signing a four-year deal in the midst of a media recession. They argue that the deal could look very cheap in three years' time should the value of football television rights rise again. They are also mindful of the fact that in 2004 the Premier League will be signing a new set of broadcast deals and that the financial gap between the Premier League and the Football League could then be exacerbated, with the Football League locked in to what could be an undervalued deal for another two years.

The Labour government promised to be a football-friendly administration and barely a week went by in the early days of its first term when a minister didn't come out as a lifelong football fan. The government promised to regulate the football business and set up the Football Task Force to that end. However, the long-awaited Independent Football Commission has been greeted with dismay by supporters as being toothless and ineffective. The Government has also to take some responsibility for the ill-fated 2006 World Cup bid and the fiasco of the national stadium, which has lowered the stock of English football's administration throughout the world.

In Europe, the Champions League, which owes its current format to the failed bid to establish a European Superleague, has become so important that domestic leagues have been all but overshadowed. But even the Champions League is suffering from falling attendances and television viewing figures. The governing body is trying to walk a fine tightrope between the needs of its 51 member federations and the big clubs, represented by the shadowy G14 group of clubs. Will the G14 clubs win out and gain automatic entry into the competition, or will they simply walk away and set up their own competition? In Chapter 7 I will show that G14's influence has been overstated but that the dynamics of the political economy of European football is leading to a *de facto* superleague, with two divisions: the top division called the Champions League and the second division named the UEFA Cup. The chapter also looks at the dilemma of the Old Firm clubs, who appear to be desperate to play anywhere except in Scotland.

The governing body of world football, FIFA, is also in the midst of a crisis that threatens its very survival. First its marketing partner ISL went bankrupt and then its media partner Kirch Group followed suit. Meanwhile, FIFA president Sepp Blatter is being investigated by his own executive committee over his handling of both issues, and questions are being asked about the way his election to the post in 1998 was achieved, amid allegations of bribery and corruption.

Just as in the 1980s football thought that satellite television would provide untold riches, the 1990s saw digital television hailed as the saviour. Neither delivered and the Internet became the medium that football thought could bail it out of its latest crisis. However, the dot.com crash not only saw sports sites go out of business, it also saw the stock market valuations of listed football clubs collapse in sympathy.

One of the commonest remedies touted for football's ills is the introduction of salary caps as favoured by American sports. However, there are serious doubts about the possibility of introducing wage caps into English or European football; not least whether such a system is consistent with European labour law. Then there are the various plans being mooted for the restructuring of the game, from regional leagues to a Premier League 2. Some argue that with around 100 professional clubs, the highest figure in Europe, there are simply too many clubs in England. Should some go semi-professional or even merge with local rivals? In Chapter 10, I will look at various proposals for both salary caps and the restructuring of English competitions.

Football is unlike any other business, not least in its inability to transform increasing income into profits. With a few notable exceptions, the majority of clubs are making losses, which are being turned into debt. Football clubs compete with each other, but unlike other businesses, they need their competitors to exist in order to thrive themselves. Football clubs have captive audiences of loyal fans, but some have taken that loyalty for granted for so long that many fans feel alienated from the clubs they have supported all their lives. There is very real danger that those fans will turn their backs on the clubs at just the time when television income is in decline and their support is most needed.

England is the home of the game, where the rules were formulated and the first clubs established. Could it be that it is in England where the fascinating story of professional football comes to its sad denouement? Or could it be that football finds the answers within the English game by returning to the first principles established over 100 years ago? This book seeks to answer that question, and address several other pertinent issues facing the game today. Football is going down, but it is not out – yet.

## ENDNOTES
[1] Manchester United plc. 26 March 2002. Interim results press briefing.

# 1. Boom and Bust

IN THE WEEK BEFORE THE 2002 WORLD CUP OPENED IN KOREA AND JAPAN THE EYES OF THE country's sports media were focused on the Far East but some highly significant events were taking place much closer to home. Indeed, at the London headquarters of the Football Association a three-man independent commission ruled that Wimbledon Football Club could move to Milton Keynes against the wishes of the supporters, the Football League and the Football Association. In Bradford, supporters of Bradford City were preparing for a public meeting that would lead to the establishment of a supporters' trust after their club had entered administration and sacked 19 of its players. Grimsby Town warned that it would go into administration unless its players agreed to take a pay-cut. Ironically the club's players were on performance-related contracts and it was Grimsby's success in avoiding relegation from the First Division that meant it was unable to pay them after the collapse of ITV Digital. In Scotland, the administrators of Motherwell were 'confident' of finding a buyer for the troubled club, but the liquidators of Airdrieonians gave up trying to save the club and it ceased to exist after 124 years. The *Financial Times* of 28 May 2002, in a story with the all too familiar headline 'Wembley Stadium's extra time could be just about to run out', claimed the long-running saga of the national stadium could be drawing to a close as the Football Association was about to sign an agreement with a German bank for the financing of a new stadium. The day before, FIFA's Scottish executive committee member David Will alleged that football's world governing body was on the verge of bankruptcy after losing £215m in the previous four years. While there may not appear to be much in common between the finances of FIFA and the location of Wimbledon, the saga of Wembley Stadium, Bradford City's slide into administration and the plight of two Scottish clubs, are illustrative of the game's malaise at a local and international level. Unsurprisingly, the stories failed to make the back or front pages of the national media, which were chiefly concerned with the fitness of England captain David Beckham. Even the *London Evening Standard* relegated the Wimbledon story to three pages in from the back page, having allocated front and back pages to Beckham and the England team.

The Wimbledon story is illustrative of football's crisis on several levels. Wimbledon Chairman Charles Koppel claimed the club was losing £20,000 a day, partly because of its status as tenant at Crystal Palace's Selhurst Park, and partly because, despite playing in the First Division, in the words of the commission: 'It carried an FA Premier League club cost base and nursed FA Premier League ambitions.' The club's plight also showed the paucity of the game's governing bodies' response to football's crisis: both the FA and Football League opposed the move but both claimed they were impotent to prevent it. The commission was at pains to point out that the decision to allow the club to relocate should not be seen as a precedent and was the result of 'exceptional circumstances'.[1] One of those 'exceptional circumstances' included losing large sums of money on an ongoing basis, a position that many English clubs had been in for a considerable length of time. Finally, the case of Wimbledon epitomises the boom-to-bust nature of recent football economics. The rise of the club from the lower reaches of the League to the top flight coincided with the inflation of football's bubble. Indeed, the sale of 80 per cent of the club by Sam Hammam to the Norwegian company AKER RGI in 1997 occurred when English football's stock was at its peak. Within five years a football club formed in 1889 was effectively out of business. Wimbledon would be moved from their south London home to a new town 50 miles away. Although the owners claimed Wimbledon would retain their identity, it is clear that the club's supporters consider their club has been effectively stolen from them and for them the club has died. In that respect the Wimbledon story also raises the question: 'What exactly is a football club?' To the Norwegian owners it is obviously a movable franchise, but to the supporters it is a historic institution firmly rooted in a community.

When Sam Hammam bought Wimbledon in 1981 he was seen as the club's saviour. Wimbledon started life as Wimbledon Old Centrals in 1889 and played on Wimbledon Common. The club moved to the Plough Lane stadium in 1912 and joined the Athenian League in 1919. Wimbledon's progress was hardly meteoric but they worked their way up through the Southern and Isthmian Leagues before being elected to the Football League. Having arrived in the football league Wimbledon gained promotion to the Third Division but found it hard to compete and were relegated back to the Fourth Division after a season. Hammam likes to tell the tale of how he was visiting his wife in hospital where a porter told him about the plight of the club he supported and the wealthy Lebanese businessman bought Wimbledon for a reported £100,000. Hammam also invested in the team and the second phase of the club's rise got underway almost immediately. Promotion to the Third Division in 1983 was followed by another promotion to the Second Division the following year. Then in 1986 the club reached the First Division after finishing third in the Second behind Norwich and Charlton. Two years later Wimbledon achieved their sporting pinnacle when they beat Liverpool at Wembley to lift the FA Cup.

As a founder member of the Premier League Wimbledon were required to convert their Plough Lane Stadium to all-seater by 1994 to comply with the Taylor Report. Hammam felt that it was unviable to renovate Plough Lane so he sold the stadium to the Safeway supermarket chain for an estimated £8.5m. Plough Lane had been given to the club by Merton Borough Council in 1959 with a covenant restricting its use to sporting events and giving the council the option to buy it back in the event of the club moving. Hammam had managed to acquire the freehold of the site by writing off £3m of debt that the club owed him in exchange and somehow managed to persuade the council to waive the restrictive covenant. He was therefore free to sell the site to the Safeway supermarket chain, pocket around £5.5m profit, and move the club to Selhurst Park on a 'temporary' basis.

Hammam was still regarded as the club's saviour so few questioned his motives. Merton Council probably thought that he would use the money to construct a new stadium somewhere, while the supporters wouldn't hear a word against the man who had brought them from the Fourth Division to the Premier League, with a win at Wembley on the way. Both have probably now considerably revised their view in the light of recent events.

Wimbledon managed to retain their Premier League status throughout the 1990s but Hammam realised that financially the club was a lost cause. The TV money that was coming in helped to mitigate against increasing player wages and the club's scouting system enabled the club to sell cheaply acquired players for handsome profits, but the underlying problem of a small fan-base meant that the figures just didn't add up. In the 1996–97 season Wimbledon earned a total of £10.41m, nearly double their earnings the previous season, thanks to the new £670m four-year TV deal with Sky. Southampton, trapped in the 15,000-capacity Dell, earned even less with a turnover of £9.24m. Newly promoted Derby County earned a little more, stuck in their non Taylor-compliant Baseball Ground. The fourth poorest club in the Premier League was Coventry City with a turnover of £12.23m, but the average Premier League club's income was £23.2m, more than double Wimbledon's. Wimbledon's attendances were also among the poorest in the Premiership with an average of 15,139 turning up to Selhurst Park, 34 more than at Southampton but 2,750 less than at Derby. The absence of its own stadium was hitting Wimbledon hard. The terms of its lease at Selhurst Park meant that it paid 10 per cent of its gate money to Altonwood Ltd, former Crystal Palace Chairman Ron Noades's holding company that owns the stadium. Wimbledon were not allowed any branding in either the stands or corporate hospitality areas, and even if they had been, all the proceeds from hospitality and catering went to Altonwood anyway. The club could not even seriously attempt to broaden its supporter base, the fundamental cause of its problems, as the lease stipulated that ticket prices could not be reduced to less than 20 per cent of the prices charged by Crystal Palace. Many clubs have sought to widen their supporter bases by offering massive discounts, Sunderland being the most successful example, but that avenue was effectively closed to Wimbledon by the terms of the lease agreed by Hammam with Noades. Southampton and Derby sought to solve their stadium problems by relocating to new purpose-built facilities – Hammam sought to solve Wimbledon's by finding two gullible Norwegians to buy the club off him for £30m.

It is not known exactly how Hammam persuaded two Norwegian multi-millionaires, Bjorn Rune Gjeslten and Kjell Inge Rokke, to buy 80 per cent of Wimbledon for a reported £25m in 1997 but that they overpaid is surely beyond doubt. The deal gave Wimbledon an implicit valuation of

£31.25m, while at the time it would have been possible to buy Leicester City for £30m or Southampton for £26m. Like Wimbledon, both clubs were in the Premier League but, unlike Wimbledon, they owned their stadia. True, Southampton would have to move to a new stadium but because they owned the freehold to The Dell the club was able to partially offset the cost by selling the land for residential development. Leicester found it difficult to expand Filbert Street but at least it had the benefit of a 20,000-plus capacity and strong fan-base so the financial consequences of playing in an inadequate stadium were not terminal. As we shall see in a later chapter, Leicester worked hard to overcome the limitations imposed by Filbert Street and many of the initiatives Leicester took were not open to Wimbledon because of the restrictions imposed by the lease at Selhurst Park. Nonetheless, a price of over £30m for a club with a small fan-base and no stadium was extremely high compared to stock-market valuations of similar clubs at the time.

The Norwegians have since said that Hammam led them to believe that a move to Dublin was on the cards. Indeed Hammam could have shown them a letter he received from Premier League Chief Executive Peter Leaver on 18 April 1997. Leaver wrote that: 'The application [to move to Dublin] was placed before the Clubs and was not objected to by any of them.'[2] However, it would not be the Premier League that decided whether or not Wimbledon could move to Dublin – the Football Association of Ireland rejected the proposed move and the next year Hammam received a letter from FA Chief Executive Graham Kelly telling him that the FA could not support a move to Dublin as the FAI had opposed it. Kelly quoted what is known as the 'Comite des nations', whereby national associations respect the decisions of others, and said that the FA could not therefore support Wimbledon in its representations to FIFA over the matter.

Just why Hammam was so keen to move to Dublin, of all places, remains a mystery. His campaign may have helped him obtain such an extortionate price from the Norwegians, but it was always going to be faced with many insurmountable hurdles, as the Old Firm clubs have found out in their attempts to move south and play in England. The FAI, UEFA, FIFA, the FA and the Premier League would all have to sanction the move. The supporters were not consulted of course, but considering their subsequent vociferous opposition to the Milton Keynes move, they would hardly be expected to embrace a move to another country.

Despite the failure of Hammam's proposed move to Dublin, he still managed to sell his remaining 20 per cent stake to Matthias Hauger and Charles Koppel for £1.5m in April 2000. Given the club's prospects of finding a new stadium at that point were at an all-time low it would seem fair to question Hauger and Koppel's motives for getting involved when they did. Certainly there was considerable hype about the forthcoming Premier League TV deal and football shares were approaching their all-time highs. Hauger and Koppel had bought 20 per cent of the club for £1.5m and compared to the Norwegians they could be forgiven for thinking that they had a bargain. However, the club was still stuck at Selhurst Park, was still losing money and was only a few games away from losing its Premier League status.

With impeccable timing, only four months after Hauger and Koppel had bought in, Koppel was approached by Peter Winkleman of the Milton Keynes Stadium Consortium who told him that the consortium was looking for a football tenant for a planned 28,000-capacity purpose-built stadium in the city. It was claimed that Milton Keynes was the largest city in Europe without a professional football team and that there was a massive potential fan-base with eight million people living within one hour's drive of the proposed stadium. The stadium would have retail developments to make it financially viable and the cost to the club would be nothing. After a series of meetings Koppel signed a deal in July 2001.

Koppel's enthusiasm for Milton Keynes betrays at best an amazing naivety about the nature of English football support and at worst a complete disregard for the game and its followers. The belief that because a city with a population of 200,000 does not have a professional team it will gladly support any club that moves there assumes that the local population doesn't already support other clubs. Local competition is provided by Luton Town, Northampton Town and Rushden and Diamonds, while Leicester City and Coventry are within an hour's drive. One would think that if there was a substantial number of people in Milton Keynes with an interest in football then they would already support a team. That said, Koppel told the commission that it was not so much the potential of Milton Keynes that was the major reason for the proposed move, rather it was 'necessary for the club's survival'.

Having signed the deal for Milton Keynes, Koppel then had to persuade the FA and the Football League to allow the move. The League has very strict rules about clubs relocating outside of the area from which they take their name and the League's board unanimously rejected the move on 16 August 2001. Koppel then appealed to the FA and a three-man panel comprising Arsenal Chief Executive David Dein, York City Chairman Douglas Craig and Charles Hollander QC met on 21 and 22 January 2002. The FA panel found that the League had reached its decision using unfair procedures and said it had rejected 'the application, not on its merits, but on the basis of an inflexible view or policy'.[3] The panel was at pains to point out that it was not considering the merits of the case but just looking at the League's way of dealing with it and, in a classic case of buck passing, referred the case back to the League to reconsider. They responded in kind and asked the FA to set up an independent commission to examine the case. What had become abundantly clear was that while the FA and the League were both opposed in principle to the move to Milton Keynes, both were afraid of any legal action that the club might take if they ruled against the relocation. There was also Koppel's threat that if the club's wish to move was denied then it would be liquidated, effectively blackmailing both bodies who would be held to have put the club out of business.

The FA then convened a Commission of Inquiry under FA rule F6 that comprised lawyer Raj Parker, Rymans League Chairman Alan Turvey and Aston Villa's Director of Operations Steve Stride. It is interesting to consider how many different groups opposed the move: the All Party Parliamentary Football Group representing 150 MPs, the Football League, the FA, Merton Borough Council, which claimed that a stadium could be built in the borough, the Football Conference and of course the Wimbledon supporters themselves, in the shape of the Wimbledon Independent Supporters Association and the Dons Trust. Against them were Charles Koppel and the Milton Keynes Stadium Consortium. In short, the FA opposed the move on sporting reasons alone, pointing out that the move would drive a coach and horses through the pyramid system whereby, in theory, any of the FA's 43,000 registered clubs could rise to the top through sporting endeavour alone. The FA also believed that clubs played a role in the communities in which they were based and that the supporters were stakeholders and as such should have a say in issues pertaining to the running of their clubs. The Football League was opposed strictly on the grounds of its rule that clubs should play within the conurbation from which they take their name. The supporters were opposed for the obvious reason that as far as they were concerned Wimbledon belonged in Wimbledon and if they couldn't have a ground in Wimbledon, then Selhurst Park, which is five miles away from Wimbledon, was preferable to a stadium more than 50 miles away. The club's case was purely financial: the club claimed to be losing £20,000 per day and there was no other viable alternative. The club would lay on subsidised travel for South London-based supporters and claimed that only 20 per cent of season-ticket holders actually lived in Merton. The club was vehement in its position that if the move was not allowed then the club would fold. If ever there was a case of football confronting business this was it. And it was no real surprise when business won.

The panel and the FA were at pains to point out the case should not be seen as a precedent, citing what they described as the 'exceptional circumstances' of the Wimbledon case – not just the horrendous finances, but also the fact the club was unique in being a secondary tenant and had not played in its own ground for 11 years. While Wimbledon's financial position was dire, it certainly is not unique and as the fallout from the collapse of ITV Digital sends more clubs into administration there is a good chance that many more clubs will be in a worse position. It is true that Wimbledon are unique in being a long-term secondary tenant, although Bristol Rovers, Charlton, Brighton and Hove Albion, Middlesbrough and Chester City have all been forced to move away from their conurbations while they resolved their own stadium issues, but whose fault is that? It should be remembered that Merton Borough Council facilitated the move to Selhurst Park by removing the restrictive covenants on the use of Plough Lane thus enabling Hammam to complete his lucrative property deal. How hard Hammam really tried to find an alternative site is unknown. It should also be remembered that Wimbledon were in this position when purchased by their current majority owners, who during their stewardship have repeatedly assured the media and the club's supporters that they were actively seeking a return to Merton, and even publicly dismissed claims that a move to Milton Keynes was on the cards. What is really hard to believe is that Charles Koppel bought into an ailing Wimbledon without any idea of how it would resolve the stadium issue. The unsolicited approach from the Milton Keynes Stadium Consortium seems just too fortuitous to be true. Whoever's fault it is that Wimbledon did not find another stadium before Milton Keynes became the only viable option, it was certainly not the club's supporters, who are the real losers in the case. The author asked Koppel to clarify these issues but he declined to reply.

To their credit, Wimbledon supporters have responded to their betrayal by the club and the authorities in an innovative and selfless manner. They have applied to the FA to register AFC Wimbledon to play in the Southern Counties League next season. An unnamed supporter wrote to the panel and his evidence was reproduced in the appendix.

> Wimbledon has no future at Milton Keynes. It will cease to exist. The name may survive for a while but the heart and soul of the club – its supporters – will be lost for ever. To all intents and purposes it will die and if that happens I believe it will represent one of the greatest betrayals in the history of football. That, of course, is for you to decide but please understand that the vast majority of supporters would prefer to see the club budget to play in a lower division – even a lower league – rather than be moved away from south London.[4]

The betrayal of Wimbledon clearly demonstrates how the competitive and regulatory structures of the game have contributed to its current crisis. The club's dire financial position post-relegation was due, as the commission identified, to the massive income gap between the Premier League and the First Division. The failure of the Football League and the Football Association to take control of the situation and stand up to Koppel and his cohorts shows just how wanting both are when faced by anyone with resources and expensive legal advice. The FA also has to take some responsibility for the income gap created by the Premier League breakaway, which it sanctioned in 1992. Both claim that the Wimbledon case was a one-off, but the paucity of their response to the situation will do little to discourage others from attempting something similar in the future.

On the face of it Bradford City's move into administration also appears to epitomise the boom-and-bust economics of modern English football. But there are also suggestions that the manipulation of this crisis has been used as an attempt to effect change in the Football League's policy towards the growing financial problems facing league clubs. The club was taken over by Geoffrey Richmond in 1994 and gained promotion to the First Division through the play-offs in 1996. Richmond made his money buying the Leeds Ronson lighter company out of administration and selling it for a handsome profit. He first bought into Scarborough FC but sold out when the opportunity to buy Bradford, then in the Second Division, presented itself. He invested in the playing squad and built a team, under the management of Chris Kamara, that was able to challenge for promotion to the First Division. In 1996 Bradford finished sixth in the Second Division and won promotion through the play-offs.

Bradford struggled to consolidate their First Division status, twice avoiding relegation on the last day of the season. However, thanks to the nature of the club's promotion from the Second Division, complete with the club's first ever Wembley appearance, average attendances at Valley Parade more than doubled to 12,925.

After their second season in the First Division, Richmond says that he looked at the fixture list and decided that it was the weakest First Division for many years and that it was worth taking a gamble in the transfer market in an audacious attempt to try and gain promotion to the top flight. Bradford then proceeded to spend £4.5m in the transfer market, twice breaking the club's transfer record with Lee Mills (£1m from Port Vale) and Isaiah Rankin (£1.3m from Arsenal). Former club hero Stuart McCall returned on a free transfer from Rangers while the former Manchester United star Lee Sharpe arrived from Leeds United. Richmond and fellow director Professor David Rhodes listed the club on the Ofex market in November 1999 in an attempt to broaden the club's ownership base, but investor sentiment towards the sector had already cooled and less than three per cent of the shares were sold.

Richmond's gamble paid off when the club gained automatic promotion to the Premiership on the last day of the season with a dramatic 3–2 win away at Wolves. Bradford had returned to the top flight after 77 years in the lower divisions, having been relegated from the First Division in 1922 along with Manchester United.

Bradford's promotion to the Premier League had a dramatic effect on the finances of the club. While it is true that promotion to the Premiership radically transforms the economics of any club, Bradford's promotion came only two years after their promotion from the Second Division. In 1996, the club's last year in the Second Division, Bradford's income was £2.96m. By 2000, Bradford's first year in the Premiership, it had reached £21.07m, itself a 170 per cent increase on the previous year's First Division income of £7.8m. Bradford have not disclosed wage figures for when they were in the Second Division, but player wages for 1999, the year of Richmond's gamble, had increased by £1.73m on the previous year to £4.04m. Although Bradford's income increased by 170 per cent on promotion to the Premiership, the increase in wages was only 68 per cent to £6.7m. The most expensive player bought was David Weatherall from Leeds United for £1.4m, while experienced Premier League players like Andy Myers, Dean Saunders and Neil Redfearn were picked up for a total of £1.55m.

After narrowly either avoiding relegation or gaining promotion in three of the four previous seasons, it was no surprise to the City faithful that Premiership survival came to be decided on the last day of the season. With Liverpool needing a victory at Valley Parade to qualify for the Champions League few gave Bradford a chance but a goal from Weatherall retained City's Premiership status and more than justified the player's £1.4m fee.

Having maintained their position in the Premiership, Richmond now embarked on what he would later call 'six weeks of madness'. Faced with manager Paul Jewell's defection to Sheffield Wednesday, he promoted Assistant Manager Chris Hutchings to the top job and set about strengthening the squad in an attempt to consolidate the club's Premier League status. Richmond quite reasonably assumed that if City had managed to survive in the top flight by spending only around £3m on new players, using some of the additional £12m income generated from that season to further strengthen the squad would result in the club finishing higher up the table and possibly challenging for a European place. In came Peter Atherton and Ian Nolan on free transfers from Sheffield Wednesday. David Hopkin was bought from Leeds United for £2.5m, while Dan Petrescu arrived from Chelsea for £1m and Ashley Ward was bought from Barnsley for £1.5m. The biggest bargain, however, was considered to be the out-of-contract Benito Carbone who cost nothing after failing to agree terms with Aston Villa. The diminutive Italian was to prove to be Richmond's Nemesis, commanding £40,000 a week on a four-year contract, a deal that was to lead to the club's plunge into administration in May 2002.

Richmond reasoned that he was able to pay Carbone £2m a year as he had saved around £2m on a transfer fee. If the gamble failed, the player could be sold as there were three years left on his contract; if it succeeded and the club stayed up, he would be well worth the money. The new additions may not have cost a lot in transfer fees, but the effect on the wage bill was staggering: up from £6.79m to £11.33m.

Richmond's biggest gamble was a spectacular failure. After a number of good results, including a victory over Chelsea and a draw with Arsenal, the team went into decline and in early November Hutchings was shown the door. Jim Jefferies came with a good reputation earned in Scotland with Heart of Midlothian, but was unable to get the side out of danger and by the New Year relegation became inevitable. It is worth pointing out at this time that Richmond paid himself and fellow directors £7.2m in dividends during the club's two-year sojourn in the Premiership, with Richmond himself pocketing over £3m. He justified the payments, the largest by far in percentage terms of any listed football club, by saying that it was an attempt to attract new investors. If that was the case it failed, as potential investors steadfastly refused to buy the shares. It could be argued that had the dividends not been paid then the money would only have been spent on more expensive players and the club's post-relegation predicament would have been even worse. However, considering that when the club went into administration it was ostensibly because it couldn't pay a £400,000 tax bill, the payments look excessive to say the least.

How much the dividend payments contributed to the club's financial collapse is arguable, but the fundamental reason for the club's predicament was the legacy of Richmond's 'six weeks of madness': a massive wage bill against greatly reduced income. Carbone and the other high-earning players were offered for loan deals or transfers but the Italian, Ward and Atherton failed to find clubs that were willing to match the earnings they were receiving at Bradford and continued to be a drain on the club's ever-decreasing resources. Meanwhile, ITV Digital went into administration and then liquidation, slashing Bradford's 2002 income by an estimated £3m. When questioned about the consequences of relegation by the *Daily Telegraph* on 24 March 2001 Richmond said: 'There is no financial problem. We are a prudently run club. We have taken steps. As and when we get relegated we go down as a strong club, not like Sheffield Wednesday or Crystal Palace. There are no problems in this club.'

It is clear, however, that whatever steps Richmond may have taken they must have included offloading the likes of Carbone and didn't allow for the collapse of ITV Digital. Carbone was loaned to Middlesbrough where he sufficiently impressed manager Steve McClaren to offer him a £25,000-a-week contract. Carbone was happy at the prospect of losing £15,000 per week but wanted a four-year contract rather than the two years that Boro were prepared to offer. Richmond received the news that Carbone's move to Middlesbrough had fallen through on the same day that he received a final demand for £400,000 from the Inland Revenue. He took out his calculator and worked out that Bradford were going to lose £10m over the following two years and were therefore technically insolvent. He immediately requested that Ofex suspend the club's shares and a week later the administrators, Kroll Buchler Phillips, were called in and ordered by a Leeds court to find a buyer for the club. A week later 19 players and 39 non-playing staff were made redundant.

As with the Wimbledon case, the story of Bradford's slide into insolvency illustrates the harsh reality of the boom-and-bust economics of English football. Bradford's promotion to the Premiership in 1999 coincided with the very height of England's football boom. A new television deal was about to be negotiated and all the signs were that it would be the most lucrative ever. In the City shares in quoted football clubs were reaching new highs, with football riding high on the tail of the dot.com boom. Against this background players were asking for ever-increasing pay deals and club chairmen, desperate to stay aboard the Premiership gravy-train were more than happy to pay. Bradford's relegation also coincided with the beginning of the deflation of football's financial bubble. The first sign was the withdrawal of NTL's offer of £328m for the Premier League's pay-per-view rights in October 2000, during Richmond's 'six weeks of madness'. By the summer of Bradford's relegation the dot.com bubble had well and truly burst and football shares were in decline. Then came the ITV Digital collapse and football was in crisis.

Although in many ways Bradford's financial difficulties typified much of the malaise in the English game, there are a number of questions about the manner of the club's decline that may only be answered in the fullness of time. Bradford's debt certainly wasn't the largest in the First Division at £14m, nor, at £11.38m, was the wage bill it inherited from the Premier League. However, turnover was depressed by the relatively small attendances at Valley Parade, which yielded just £4.6m in gate receipts and season-ticket sales in the year to June 2001, the last for which figures are available. Bradford's total share of the Premier League TV deal was £10.04m and with £4.5m earned from sponsorship, merchandising and other sources total revenue was around £18m. There was a feeling in some quarters that Bradford's administration was in some way contrived to force a showdown with the PFA and make the League revise its insolvency policy. The League has a policy that all football debts must be honoured in order for a club to participate in the League. That means clubs that go into administration must pay all outstanding debts to other clubs, for transfers, and to players for the remainder of their contracts, before they can be included in the fixture list. Former FA Chief Executive Graham Kelly wrote in *The Independent* that he thought Bradford's administration was part of a strategy of mass administration, first suggested to a meeting of the Football League's commercial committee, of which Richmond was a member, on 3 May by Tottenham Non-executive Chairman David Buchler, a partner in the insolvency company Kroll Buchler Phillips, that was later appointed as administrators at Bradford.

Buchler's suggested strategy was to use the dispute between the League and ITV Digital as a means of changing the League's insolvency policy to allow the mass sacking of players, which would lead to direct confrontation with the PFA. Buchler was confident that any legal challenge by the PFA would not stand up in court. On 8 June 2002 Buchler told the *Financial Times*: 'Unless the League's policy is changed, clubs will be powerless to restructure their costs. Clubs should have the right to renegotiate contracts, but under the League's policy they don't.'

When Buchler presented his strategy to a meeting of League chairmen on 17 May, the day after Bradford entered administration, it was rejected and his services as an advisor were dispensed with. On 24 May, the day after Bradford sacked 19 players, the League wrote to each club to restate its insolvency policy. 'The board took the view that the rules are in place to protect sporting principles and the League's competitions.' The letter pointed out that other clubs had been through the administrative process and had 'emerged stronger than before'. It would uphold its insolvency policy so that Bradford would not gain a competitive advantage over other clubs by signing high-costing players and then reneging on their contracts while other clubs had to meet those contracts in full. As reported in *The Independent* of 17 June 2002, the League continued:

To refuse to honour contracts relating to those players and terminating in this way the club will have retained their status without the expense under the contracts going forward, in contrast to those clubs that run their affairs in a more sensible manner and structure contractual provisions relating to length and remuneration in accordance with prudent business practice.

Richmond resigned from the Football League board the same day.

If Bradford's administration was part of a strategy to confront the PFA and challenge both the legality of players' contracts and the League's insolvency policy, it failed. When, to no surprise, Richmond was unveiled as having bought the club back from the administrators, he addressed the fans on a platform with the PFA's Chief Executive Gordon Taylor. The PFA had made available a £1m loan to the club in order that it could continue to pay the players, and further funds were available. The League's insolvency policy and the security of players' contracts remained intact.

The football authorities' inability to make a stand on the Wimbledon case, with the buck being passed from the Football League to the FA and back again, before reaching an almost universally unpopular decision, on which there is no appeal, should come as no surprise. The FA in particular has shown itself to be adept at ducking the major issues facing the game and nothing epitomises its indecisiveness more than the fiasco that is Wembley. The famous Twin Towers currently stand derelict in north London as a monument to the FA's vanity and uselessness. It should be remembered that the main reason for the rebuilding of Wembley as a national stadium was that it formed the centrepiece of England's ill-conceived and ultimately futile bid to host the 2006 World Cup. When England played their last game at the venue against Germany, the kick-off was delayed by half an hour because of transport delays. German television thoroughly enjoyed the delay as it gave the presenters half an hour to pour scorn on the unsuitability of the venue to host World Cup matches and the amateurism of the FA's organisation of the event. Of course, England lost, with Kevin Keegan finally realising what half the country had known for ages: that he just wasn't up to the job. Senior FA officials duly tried to persuade him to stay but thankfully his mind was made up and he resigned straight after the game. The story of the FA and Wembley will be recounted in detail in Chapter 8 but the saga illustrates how the governing body has become caught up in football's boom-and-bust economics. The original cost of the project was £230m, which has risen to £715m in five and a half years. The original financiers were the American bank Chase Manhattan, who in 2000 attempted to raise £400m in syndicated loans from other City institutions but failed to do so as sentiment towards the project in particular, and football in general, had cooled considerably. Similarly, by the time Barclays was appointed lead bank late in 2001, the global financial crisis had led to banks being much more stringent in their lending and the FA's failure to provide answers to the bank's questions led to Barclays withdrawing as well, to be replaced by the German bank West LB.

The Wembley saga is another telling example of how the FA has failed in its governance of the game and although it has sought to blame everyone but itself for all the delays that have dogged the project, it is hard to see who else is responsible. The government and Sport England have contributed to the project and, not unreasonably, have called the FA to account. The FA has alternated between distancing itself from the project and trying to take a lead, insisting at some stages that the stadium be used exclusively for football and at others refusing to countenance the building of a cheaper alternative at another location. The FA has shown itself to be woefully inadequate in governing the game during its recent boom, and there must therefore be serious doubts about its ability to oversee the game's financial crisis.

The finances of FIFA, the world governing body, may not, on the face of it, seem to be linked to those of the English game, but one of the contributory factors to the £215m shortfall that David Will brought to the world's attention before the World Cup was the collapse of the German media company Kirch Group, who held the rights to the 2002 and 2006 World Cup finals. The collapse of Kirch also had a devastating effect on the finances of German football where the Bundesliga was left at least £60m short in a scenario very similar to that of ITV Digital and the Football League. However, the Kirch collapse will have a long-term effect on the value of all European football TV rights as it removes one of the major players and reduces competition. If, as seems likely, Rupert Murdoch or Silvio Berlusconi, or both in partnership, emerge as the dominant pay-TV broadcaster in Germany, it will give them control of three of Europe's top five pay-TV markets. That would mean that the value of the TV rights to the Champions League would probably fall, which in turn could have a serious effect on the bottom line of some of England's biggest clubs.

Of more concern to English clubs, however, are FIFA's attempts to take control of European club football. FIFA used to be mainly concerned with its primary revenue driver, the World Cup, but has viewed with alarm the rise in the economic power of Europe's top clubs. The ill-fated World Club Championship was a pathetic attempt to give FIFA a cash cow to rival the UEFA's Champions League. The FA's shameless support of the event, sanctioning Manchester United's withdrawal from the FA Cup in order that it compete in the inaugural 1999 competition in the misguided belief that it would help England's 2006 World Cup campaign, shows how the FA will put its own narrowly perceived self interest before that of the domestic game. FIFA's attempts to control domestic club football have had an immediate effect on the crisis in the Football League. Ostensibly, the internationally coordinated fixture calendar tried to put an end to the continuing club v. country struggle as increasingly international club squads were regularly undermined by the demands of a myriad of international tournaments. However, part of the calendar was the imposition of transfer windows in all leagues. With Football League clubs faced with massive uncertainty following the ITV Digital collapse, many needed to trim their squads and looked to sell players in order to balance the books. The imposition of transfer windows, allowing clubs only to trade players in the close season and for a month in December and January, seriously reduces clubs' options in this respect. Indeed the Football League's leadership has pointed out that if FIFA's transfer-window system had been in place from last year, Nottingham Forest would not have been able to sell Jermaine Jenas to Newcastle United for £5m and would probably have gone into administration. Another way that FIFA has had a direct influence on the current crisis is in its role in talks with the European Union over the rules governing international transfers. The agreed rules, which were opposed by most English clubs, give even more power to players, allowing them to walk out on clubs mid-contract on the pretext of 'just sporting cause'. While the case of Jenas at Forest would not come under the new rules, as it was a wholly domestic transfer, the general effect of the rules is to continue the post-Bosman trend away from transfer fees to higher player wages. Since the Bosman ruling, English League clubs have found it harder to balance their books through selling players developed through their youth systems to larger clubs.

Football's crisis is truly global and extends from the lower reaches of the Football League, where Halifax Town entered administration on relegation from the Football League to the Football Conference, to FIFA, by way of Italy's Serie A, where the 18 clubs made a combined loss of £82.3m in the 2000–01 season. The global nature of the crisis means that it requires a global solution but the re-election of Sepp Blatter as president of FIFA means that it is unlikely to be forthcoming. In England, the Football Association has done nothing to suggest that it is even aware of the nature of the crisis, let alone that it has any ideas as to how to confront it. The Football League has so far restricted itself to taking legal action in order to force Carlton and Granada to pay the money owed by their failed joint venture, ITV Digital, although if it relaxes its rigid insolvency policy then it will have shown that it is at least taking the crisis seriously.

It is not enough just to say that football is in crisis, it needs to be understood how that crisis has come about. Only once that is understood will the game be able to make the reforms that are needed not only for it to survive the current crisis, but to ensure that it avoids further crises in the future. The factor most often quoted as responsible for football's current financial crisis is a fall in the value of TV rights, but I shall argue that this is only a very small part of the problem. In the case of English football, the collapse of ITV Digital has exposed the structural deficiencies of the sport. That the collapse of a nascent television platform can wreak such havoc on a game that has survived for well over 100 years surely suggests that there is something seriously wrong with the relationship between football and television.

That football has a problem with television is hardly surprising as its regulatory and competitive structures were formed in the nineteenth century when the economy in which football operated was totally different to that of today. Football clubs themselves have changed into businesses, albeit unique ones, but while the FA and the Football League have developed their commercial operations to exploit sponsorship and television markets, they have largely maintained their nineteenth-century political structures. The Football Association remains ruled by its 92-member council, representing both the amateur and professional game, with councillors voting on behalf of groups as diverse as the universities and the armed services. The Football League remains representative of the clubs, or more particularly their chairmen, with a voting structure based on membership. Both bodies have boards made up of members, who oversee an appointed executive. Inevitably there are conflicts between the FA and the Football League and indeed the formation of the third part of the competitive and regulatory structure of the English game was a product of that conflict. The formation of the Premier League in 1992 added a new governing body with a smaller constituency, but with more economic power, than the Football Association and Football League. The Premier League, for all its newness, retained a similar structure to the Football League and unsurprisingly is subject to the same internal political tensions and dynamics and has also entered the power struggle between the Football Association and the League.

While the governing bodies have changed little structurally since the nineteenth century, the same cannot be said of the clubs. Indeed, as the next chapter shows, they have changed into businesses largely to take advantage of the opportunities afforded by television. This change has further exacerbated the tensions between the clubs and the governing bodies, which are at the heart of football's current crisis.

## ENDNOTES

1 Football Association. 2002. *Decision on the matter of Wimbledon FC and the proposed move to Milton Keynes*: 5.

2 Ibid.

3 Ibid.

4 Ibid.

# 2. Football as a Business

THAT FOOTBALL IS A BUSINESS IS NOW BEYOND ANY DOUBT. CLUBS ARE QUOTED ON THE STOCK market and turn over millions of pounds a year. Clubs' commercial departments sign multi-million-pound deals with sponsors, caterers, kit suppliers and corporate-hospitality companies. Away from the clubs, whole sectors have grown to service the 'industry'. Top law firms and merchant banks have sports departments, whose most lucrative work derives from the football sector. Similarly, agencies specialising in selling football media rights have become multi-million-pound companies themselves as the value of the rights they trade has continued to rise. Some players' agents have also become quoted companies as the value of the contracts they negotiate on their clients' behalf become ever more lucrative.

Although football is a business, it is almost a unique one and differs from other businesses in a number of highly significant ways. Firstly, there is the relationship between competing clubs. In most businesses there is a natural tendency to either take over or force out of business rivals for customers, but football clubs need other clubs in order to provide competition. Secondly, there is the relationship between the club and the supporter, or customer. Supporters sometimes seem loyal beyond reason and will not support another club just because it is performing better on the pitch or is charging lower admission prices. This nature of football support, as a captive market, is what attracts sponsors and marketers to the sport. Fan loyalty is double-edged however: mergers or relocation may make sound business sense to some clubs, but supporter opposition is often an insurmountable barrier. However, the most fundamental difference between football and mainstream business is its attitude to profit. When Tottenham Hotspur's Finance Director John Sedgwick announced to an analysts' briefing in 1999 that the club was no longer going to pay a dividend to shareholders, he said: 'Football clubs should not make a profit as such but should invest any surplus in team strengthening.'[1] The inability of quoted clubs to make profits or pay dividends will be covered in-depth in Chapter 3, but the uniqueness of football as a business in its attitude to profits and dividends can be illustrated by the fact that since the rush to the stock market in 1997 and 1998 few clubs have consistently made profits and even those that have, have paid mainly insignificant dividends.

Another way that football is different from any other business is the regulatory and competitive structure within which it operates. Like all businesses, football clubs have to abide by the laws of the land, but they also have to comply with a number of other regulatory constraints imposed by the governing bodies. In England, clubs are governed by the rules of either the Football or Premier Leagues, as well as those of the Football Association, UEFA and FIFA. What follows is an attempt to show how the first two of those have shaped the economic environment in which the English game now operates. As one of the main conclusions of this book is that the current crisis in the English game is in part due to structural deficiencies and that an overhaul of the way the game is governed is necessary, it is important to understand how the structural and operating environment has evolved.

The game that we know as football became formalised with the foundation of the Football Association in 1863. The Association was formed in order to agree a set of rules to facilitate matches between various sports clubs, who had previously played local variations of a game which had its roots in 'folk football' going back to at least the fourteenth century. As explained by Dave Russell in *Football and the English*, the sport had risen to prominence in the early nineteenth century and moved from the public schools as former pupils sought to play the game of their youth in adulthood. Each public school had its own particular variant of the game with the main points of difference being the use of the hands and levels of physical contact. The Association became split into two separate camps: those who favoured the kicking game and those who preferred the handling game. The schools at Marlborough, Rugby and Cheltenham preferred the latter while Eton, Shrewsbury and Westminster were among those who championed the former. After a series of meetings a vote was held on 8 December 1863 and the kickers won the day by 13 votes to 4. Association Football, or soccer as it then became known (soccer being slang for association), was thus born.[2]

In the early days of the Football Association the sport was mainly the preserve of the upper classes as evidenced by the first winners of the FA Cup, The Wanderers, a team whose membership was exclusively made up of former public school pupils and Oxbridge graduates. In fact, in the first ten years of the FA Cup, the tournament was dominated by The Wanderers, who won it five times in the 1870s. Old Etonians won the Cup twice, before losing the 1883 final to the professional northern team Blackburn Olympic, who went on to become Blackburn Rovers. The Old Etonians victory in 1882 was the last by an amateur team and marked the end of the gentleman amateur era.

Russell identifies the 1870s as the period when the game spread from the upper and middle classes to the working masses. A general rise in incomes during that period was accompanied by an increase in leisure time and the government passed a law in 1874 that gave most workers Saturday afternoon off. The free Saturday afternoon not only facilitated the arrangement of fixtures, but also created an audience to watch matches. There were many other developments during the mid- to late-nineteenth century that helped the game grow — the rise of the media and the development of the railway system for example — but economic growth and a rise in leisure time were crucial.

The second half of the nineteenth century saw the establishment of many of the clubs that now dominate the modern game. Football was adopted by some pre-existing cricket clubs so that the clubs could continue to function during the winter months. Others were founded by churches, such as Everton and Southampton, while some were grounded in the workplace, like Manchester United, whose first members were employees of the Newton Heath railway works, and Arsenal, which drew from workers at the Royal Woolwich Arsenal. When looking at the structure of the modern game, it is very important to understand that the clubs very often pre-dated both the FA and the Football League. This is why the adoption of the American models for sports such as baseball and American football, with clubs franchised by the sports' governing bodies, is inappropriate for English football where the clubs are sovereign. The origins of the Football League emphasise this point: the body was formed in 1888 to organise matches between clubs that were already established as professional football clubs after a sometimes acrimonious debate about professionalism within the sport that ran throughout the mid-1880s.

The origins of professionalism are difficult to study, not least because prior to its authorisation by the FA in 1885 it was carried out clandestinely, and also because some payments to players were authorised by the FA's Rule 16 from 1882. Rule 16 allowed payment for travelling expenses and compensation for loss of earnings incurred when players participated in the FA Cup. Between 1882 and 1885 there were many disputes where amateur teams, mainly from the south, complained that their northern opponents were in breach of Rule 16 by overpaying some players' expenses. The breach of Rule 16 which provoked the most objections, however, was the practice of offering inducements, usually in the form of local employment, to attract players to a particular club. As Russell notes, many Scottish players were attracted to Lancashire clubs such as Preston North End and Burnley by local job offers, with Preston able to secure the services of Blackburn Olympic's George Wilson by offering him the tenancy of the Black-Moor-Head public house. Preston North End were thrown out of the FA Cup in 1884 after London amateur side Upton Park complained to the FA that the club was to all intents and purposes professional. Burnley were excluded from the next FA Cup before it even got underway and by the autumn professional clubs hit back by threatening a breakaway British Football Association.

The FA's response to the first of many breakaway threats became its response to practically every crisis it subsequently had to face: it set up a committee. With 31 clubs now pressing for professionalism to be legalised, the scale of the breakaway threat demanded a measured response and in July 1885 the FA allowed clubs to employ players, with certain restrictions. Some of the restrictions, such as professional players having to have either been born or resided locally for two years, were designed to stem the rise of professionalism, while others, such as the registration of players, the establishment of the maximum wage and the foundation of the retain-and-transfer system, were sought by the professional clubs to secure the services of their players. Although there have been many changes to the rules since, most notably the scrapping of the residency restrictions and the maximum wage, the compromise of 1885 established the framework for the professional game.

The legalisation of professionalism brought with it a need for a more lucrative competitive structure for the game. Clubs had invested in stadia and players but were limited to playing FA Cup ties or friendlies – although they had regular outgoings in terms of wages, they couldn't be sure of regular cash-generative fixtures. The issue was addressed at a series of meetings between the clubs in 1888 and on 17 April of that year the League was formed comprising 12 clubs: Accrington, Aston Villa, Blackburn Rovers, Bolton Wanderers, Burnley, Derby County, Everton, Notts County, Preston North End, Stoke, West Bromwich Albion and Wolverhampton Wanderers. A second division was also formed but folded after a season and various other regional leagues were formed in the late nineteenth century, most notably the Southern League in 1892.

It is important to emphasise at this point that although the game was professional with a concomitant competitive structure by the beginning of the twentieth century, the clubs themselves were not run as businesses in the broad sense of the word. Following the legalisation of professionalism in 1888, Small Heath, later to become Birmingham City, were the first club to become a limited liability company. Many soon followed suit and the FA responded by creating its Rule 34 in 1896 that limited the payment of dividends to directors to 5 per cent of profits. The rule also stipulated that directors could not draw a salary and that if a club was wound up any surplus would be distributed to local sporting clubs. The rule was relaxed in 1981, increasing the allowed dividend payment to 15 per cent and allowing a director to draw a salary as long as he worked full time. The reason why the rule was relaxed was ostensibly to facilitate more professional management of clubs and encourage investment. However, one part of the rule was still in place: the subsection concerning the distribution of assets on winding up, which was proving to be an impediment to stock-market flotation. The purpose of this subsection was to guard against asset stripping, but it was circumvented by the creation of parent companies that were outside of the FA's jurisdiction. This expedient was first utilised by Tottenham Chairman Irving Scholar in 1981 who managed to take Spurs to the stock market despite the remaining restrictions of Rule 34. Scholar created a holding company of which the football club was a subsidiary. The holding company was outside of the FA's jurisdiction and could therefore pay dividends and director's salaries. The legitimacy of Scholar's model was not challenged by the FA, as Scholar revealed at a later date: 'We wrote to them and said we were thinking of doing it that way. I don't remember receiving a reply.'[3]

Faced with growing criticism that it had abandoned some of its founding principles by not enforcing Rule 34, the FA responded by quietly dropping the subsections of the rule limiting dividends and directors' salaries at its summer council meeting of 1998. As Nic Coward, the FA's Head of Regulation put it: 'As the rules weren't working, there was no point keeping them.'[4] That response is somewhat disingenuous as the reason the rules weren't working was because the FA did not enforce them.

Although two subsections of Rule 34 were scrapped, the one pertaining to the winding up of clubs and the redistribution of their assets remained in place. However, it is unclear whether or not that part of the rule can be circumvented by the experiment of the holding company. In 2002 there was nearly an opportunity to find out when York City Chairman Douglas Craig threatened to close down the club and sell its Bootham Crescent ground, owned by holding company Bootham Crescent Holdings, for housing development, netting Craig and his cohorts a profit of around £3.5m. Thankfully motor-racing entrepreneur John Batchellor bought the club from the directors and the future of the club has been secured – at least for the time being. That the FA saw fit to appoint Craig to a panel to discuss Wimbledon's plans to relocate to Milton Keynes while he was trying to close down York for personal gain still defies reason.

The changes to Rule 34 allowed clubs to float on the stock market, which radically changed their nature both as sporting institutions and businesses. There is more than a little irony in the fact that Rule 34 was designed to limit dividends, yet since its circumvention has been tolerated by the FA, very few quoted clubs have managed to pay worthwhile dividends, certainly not in excess of the stipulated 15 per cent of profits. In fact few have made any profits at all.

Although prior to the 1980s few directors made money directly from their clubs, many did through contracts for the supply of goods and services. In the late 1950s and 1960s Burnley Chairman Bob Lord led a campaign against televised football because of the perceived effect it would have on attendances and consequently on the sales of the meat pies that Lord's company supplied to the club. Other directors were happy to be associated with their local clubs because of the prestige and profile that accrued. Few, it would appear, were motivated simply by the desire to make money. Thus for the first eight decades of the twentieth century football clubs were run in much the same way as they had been at the end of the nineteenth. They may have been limited companies but there the similarities with mainstream businesses ended. Even the treatment of players was anachronistic. The banning of the maximum wage in 1961 and the Bosman ruling of 1995 merely gave footballers some of the rights that most other employees had enjoyed for decades.

English football was dragged into the twentieth-century business culture in the 1980s by a combination of events; the Bradford City fire disaster being the first and one of the most tragic. When Bradford played Lincoln City on the last day of the 1984–85 season, 11,076 supporters went to Valley Parade to celebrate winning the Third Division Championship, the club's first title for 56 years. Celebrations were short-lived, however, as a fire broke out under the main stand shortly before the end of the first half. Referee Don Shaw took the players off the pitch as the fire quickly spread the length of the antiquated wooden stand. Thousands managed to escape to safety by evacuating on to the pitch, but those who tried to exit through the back of the stand found some gates locked and 56 people lost their lives with a further 265 injured. An inquiry revealed that the fire was probably started by a discarded match or cigarette which had dropped into a void below the seats that was filled with rubbish accumulated over the years. Although there is no doubt that the fire was a tragic accident, the dilapidated state of the stadium was a contributory factor. The subsequent government inquiry led by Mr Justice Popplewell proposed new legislation governing safety at the nation's sports grounds and stadia, especially lower divisions' antiquated wooden stands that had been in use for decades. It is worth stating at this point that one vital lesson from the Bradford fire disaster remained unlearned. Popplewell noted in his report: 'The importance of allowing full access to the pitch where this is likely to be used as a place of safety in an emergency should be made plain.' Sadly perimeter fences remained at most English grounds and made a highly significant contribution to the Hillsborough Disaster four years later in which 95 supporters were crushed to death.

The 1989 Hillsborough Disaster had even more profound consequences for English football than the Bradford fire. The subsequent Taylor Report, which was the ninth such report into crowd safety, was the most far-reaching study into the state of the game. Among the recommendations of the report was a call for all grounds to be all-seater by the end of the millennium. Football therefore had to find money to implement this recommendation which was published in 1990. The Government reduced the tax on football pools, diverting £100m to ground development over the next five years, while the Football Trust contributed £40m over the same period. Total spending on stadia in all divisions reached £417m by 1996, with £292m spent by Premier League clubs.

The first football club to float on the stock market was Tottenham Hotspur in 1983. The club had become burdened with debt and was taken over by Irving Scholar, who was a pioneer in the football business in that he devised a strategy that placed the football club at the centre of a number of businesses, from sportswear manufacturing to corporate hospitality and publishing. Scholar was one of the first of a new breed of entrepreneur who believed that it was possible to make money out of football but he found the traditional structure of the club, with the concomitant restrictions on dividends, a serious impediment to his plans. Scholar circumvented the FA's rules, specifically Rule 34, by forming a holding company of which the football club would be a subsidiary. With the new structure in place Tottenham Hotspur plc was floated on the stock market on 13 October 1983 raising £3.8m. Although the flotation was a success in that the offer was four times oversubscribed and the club's debts were wiped out, the company struggled to make any profits and was plunged into crisis after the over-ambitious acquisition of the sportswear brand Hummel in 1991. The company was eventually bought by Alan Sugar and Terry Venables, a partnership that ended in acrimony and legal action in 1993.

The second club to float on the stock market was an unmitigated success in both sporting and business terms and has served as a template for the industry throughout the 1990s. Manchester United is commonly referred to as 'the richest club in the world' and in terms of income it certainly has been. When the club joined the stock market in 1991 it only did so because majority shareholder Martin Edwards had failed in his bid to sell his majority shareholding in the club to Michael Knighton for £10m. Edwards had inherited his stake from his father Louis, a Manchester butcher who accumulated shares during the '60s and '70s. Edwards junior floated the club in June 1991 at 385p per share, valuing the club at £47m, and immediately sold £6m worth of stock, leaving him with a 28 per cent stake. Edwards gradually reduced his holding over the following decade, and by May 2002 had sold all but 172,000 of his shares, the last tranche being 17 million shares for around £20m to mining and property magnate Harry Dobson, who said, 'It is the best value stock in an out-of-favour sector'. Indeed, the price that Dobson paid was around 127p per share, compared to the all time high the stock had reached just two years previously. In 1992, the shares were worth the equivalent of 14p each.

Manchester United's entry to the stock market was fortuitously timed in that it coincided with the formation of the Premier League and the beginning of United's domination of domestic football. Winning the FA Cup in 1991 is generally perceived to have saved Manager Alex Ferguson from the sack and started a remarkable run of form that saw the club win seven of the first ten Premiership titles. United's success on the pitch was matched by an impressive financial performance off it, reflected in the share price, rising from 14p in 1992 to 150p by December 1996. It is hardly surprising then that by 1997, with the new £670m Premier League TV deal in place, other clubs were keen to follow. However, commercially there is only one Manchester United.

The building block upon which Manchester United has constructed its commercial success has been its Old Trafford stadium. For all the talk of merchandising and TV rights, it is the paying spectator that has been the cornerstone of the club's success. Work on making Old Trafford Taylor-compliant commenced in 1992 and between 1993 and 1996 over £32.5m was spent. Throughout the building work, the stadium still managed to have the greatest capacity in English football and as each part of the stadium was refurbished admission prices also increased. In 2001 gate receipts totalled £46.2m, more than the total turnover of Sunderland, the club with the eighth highest turnover in the Premiership, and accounted for 36 per cent of the club's income. That figure came from 27 home games with an average League attendance of 67,100, over 20,000 more than the next highest-attended club, Newcastle United. Obviously, it would have been pointless building the country's largest stadium if there were not sufficient fans to fill it but that has never been a problem for United. Even when the club was relegated in 1974, their average Second Division attendance was 48,389, 2,423 more than Liverpool, the best-supported club in the First Division. The refurbishment of Old Trafford was not, then, a gamble in the same way that the building of Sunderland's Stadium of Light was, where the club has had to work hard with offers and promotions to fill the stadium.

Much of United's commercial success has been attributed to its merchandising operation which had sales of £21.9m in 2001. Although the figure is impressive, and more than double that of United's nearest rival, it should be remembered that it includes purchasing and retailing costs. Merchandising, of which sales of replica shirts is the major part, is what is termed a low-margin revenue stream with the profit margin considerably lower than that of high-margin streams such as sponsorship and television, which incur much lower costs. It is interesting to note that United are moving towards a licensing system for their merchandising whereby the club collects a royalty on goods sold by a third party, rather than buying goods, adding the United brand and then selling them on for a profit. The licensed model is favoured by continental clubs because it removes the risk of being left holding unsold stock, which can have a devastating effect on profitability.

So, although Manchester United was no doubt a commercially well-run and astute club, its financial success owed less to the club being quoted on the stock exchange than being in the right place (the top of the Premier League) at the right time (the first half of the 1990s). That said, the rush of flotations that occurred in 1996 and 1997 probably had less to do with club chairmen trying to emulate United's financial success by adopting a similar ownership model, than it did with them trying to emulate Martin Edwards and cashing in their stakes at the top of the market. As David Conn pointed out in *The Football Business,* the only people who appear to have benefited from the mass of flotations of 1996–97 are the directors who took their clubs to the market. In doing so their stakes were given values considerably in excess of what they paid for them. In 1997 Conn showed how 'football's fat cats' had benefited from the rush to the stock market: Martin Edwards had invested £600,000 in Manchester United which was worth £74m; Sir John Hall and his family invested £3m in Newcastle United and saw their stake valued at £102m within eight years; while Aston Villa's Doug Ellis paid £500,000 for his share of Aston Villa which was worth £37m following the club's 1997 flotation.

The rush to the stock market of 1996–97 started with Chelsea in March followed by Leeds United in August the same year. Sunderland, Aston Villa and Newcastle United followed, and by the end of 1997, 18 English clubs were quoted on either the main stock market or the junior Alternative Investment Market with Arsenal's shares traded on the less-regulated Ofex market. The ownership structure of English football had been transformed. The old model of a sporting club in which a few thousand people held a few worthless shares in a limited company that never made a profit had been replaced by public-quoted companies with institutional and wealthy individual shareholders. The change in the ownership structure led to a change in business objectives and strategy. Shareholders demanded returns in the shape of dividends or a growth in the value of their investments. Shares in football clubs were originally touted as 'growth stocks' which investors bought for their potential for capital growth rather than for earnings from dividends. As we shall see, at first the value of football club shares grew in line with the rest of the stock market before a steep rise in 1999 when BSkyB bid for Manchester United. After that bid was blocked by the Office of Fair Trading, football shares continued to rise as negotiations for the 2001 Premier League TV deal got more intense, while at the same time football got caught up in the dot.com boom. As share values were rising shareholders were happy to forgo dividends, hence the quote from Sedgwick at the start of this chapter, in return for capital growth. However, when values started to fall in 2000, shareholders were left wondering whether football clubs would ever make any profits and pay dividends. Looking at the prospect of shrinking television revenues and the inability of clubs to control player wage inflation, the answer they got was an emphatic 'No'.

The quoted clubs represented a cross section of the English game. There were Premier League clubs with a tradition of success like Manchester United, Arsenal, Leeds United, Chelsea, Newcastle United and Aston Villa. There were the sleeping giants, clubs with heritage but who had recently underperformed: Sunderland and Bolton Wanderers could be classed in this category, as could Preston North End. There were clubs that had spent many seasons in the top flight, but also many below that, such as Sheffield United and Leicester City. The new business culture also spread to clubs without a stock market listing but which had attracted institutional investment: Sheffield Wednesday with Charterhouse and Derby County with Apax Partners are examples where the ownership of clubs was widened to include financial institutions without recourse to the stock market. In many cases where venture capital was invested in football clubs during the rush to the stock market of 1996–97, the medium-term strategy was to exit when the club was floated on the market. Those funds that invested with that strategy in mind found that when they were expecting to realise their investment the market in football shares had fallen so sharply that a successful flotation was an impossibility. As a result much of the money that was invested during football's gold rush remained reluctantly locked in.

Although there was a massive shift in the ownership of many English football clubs in the latter half of the 1990s, the actual political power within the game remained in the same hands as previously. It is possible to retain control of a club without actually owning all the shares in it. For example Ken Bates only owns 17.7 per cent of Chelsea but because he has the support of Chelsea's largest shareholder, Swan Management – an off-shore trust that owns 26.3 per cent of the club – he has effective control and represents the club on various FA committees. Likewise Aston Villa Chairman Doug Ellis only owns 33.6 per cent of the club but no one doubts his control. However, there have been some significant changes in the control of clubs during the 1990s, some more subtle than others. At Manchester United Martin Edwards' gradual sale of his inherited stake saw his influence decrease accordingly. After the blocked sale of the club to BSkyB, which would have netted Edwards £80m, Edwards said he would reduce his 17 per cent further if it would enable him to become chairman after the planned retirement of plc Chairman Sir Roland Smith. In the event Smith stayed on for another year which gave investors sufficient time to find Roy Gardener who, with a background of running the utilities company Centrica, formerly British Gas, was used to dealing with a broad shareholder base. The biggest single shareholder in Manchester United now is BSkyB with 9.9 per cent of the shares; the rest are split between a number of institutions and wealthy individuals. Some chairmen, like Newcastle United's Sir John Hall, only sold a minority stake to the market and remained majority shareholders after flotation, while some, like Nottingham Forest and Leicester City, were the subject of bitter takeover battles, the fallout from which would haunt them for years.

The investment community's faith in football as displayed in the rush to the stock market of 1996–97 seemed to be vindicated by the events of autumn 1998 when BSkyB made its bid for Manchester United. In August of that year *The Guardian* ran a front-page story that claimed BSkyB was about to make a bid for Tottenham Hotspur. The story mentioned the concept of vertical integration, which was another way of saying that football rights were becoming so valuable to broadcasters that rather than just buy the rights, media companies might as well buy the football clubs that owned them. The reason it was felt that clubs would soon be bought by media companies was that negotiations for the sale of Premier League TV rights from 2001 were due to start the following year. It was argued that interested bidders would buy clubs so as to at least give themselves a seat at the tables or even be able to effectively negotiate the sale of the rights to themselves.

In the history of English professional football BSkyB's bid for Manchester United in late 1998 remains a landmark. The proposed deal brought to the fore the simmering uneasiness that many close to the game felt about the increasing corporatism in the sport. There is an argument that had a media company other than BSkyB bid for United there would not have been the same level of opposition. Certainly it is true that Rupert Murdoch had become something of an ogre amongst football fans who saw Sky as being responsible for the increasing commercialism of the game. There was also Murdoch's ownership of *The Sun* newspaper, never forgiven for its portrayal of Hillsborough victims as drunks, and his strategy of smashing the unions at News International.

Soon after BSkyB made its offer to buy Manchester United, cable company NTL made a bid for Newcastle United and in doing so showed that it was going to be a serious player for Premier League TV rights. When the BSkyB/Manchester United deal was referred to the Monopolies and Mergers Commission (MMC), NTL announced that it would not proceed with its purchase of Newcastle United if the Commission blocked the deal. This demonstrated that NTL was shadowing BSkyB – it had no intention of owning and running football clubs, it merely wanted to make sure it would have some content for its expanding network.

When the MMC launched its investigation into the proposed BSkyB/Manchester United deal many observers thought the deal would be allowed, perhaps with some restrictions placed on the broadcaster. That the deal was blocked owed much to the tireless campaigning of the Independent Manchester United Supporters Association and the small shareholders group Shareholders United. At the same time as the MMC were examining the case, the Restrictive Practices Court (RPC) was also considering the Office of Fair Trading's assertion that the collective selling of Premier League TV rights was 'uncompetitive'. Because of uncertainty surrounding the possible outcome of the RPC case, the MMC preferred to focus on BSkyB's position as the dominant force in British pay television and found that if the deal was allowed, that dominance would be reinforced. It was also accepted by the MMC that the deal would further cement United's dominance of English football and for those two reasons the MMC ruled against the merger. Sky's Director of Sport, Vic Wakeling, claimed after the ruling that it was a 'sad day for football' and that United would not be able to compete with other top European clubs. Later that year United won the treble of the Premier League, FA Cup and the European Cup.

Once the MMC had ruled against the BSkyB/Manchester United deal, the media companies retreated to a fall-back position. BSkyB had already acquired around 11 per cent of United's shares and indicated that it would retain its stake. In August 1999, Sky announced that it was to take a 9.9 per cent stake in Leeds United, in return for a role as exclusive commercial rights agent. Sky's deal with Leeds, and all subsequent partnerships the company formed with other clubs, gave Sky the right to market those commercial rights that were not sold centrally by the Premier League, the FA, the Football League or UEFA, in return for a share of the proceeds. In practice this meant the broadcaster would sell the rights to the UEFA Cup and sponsorship deals, and retain 30 per cent of the proceeds. Some Leeds United shareholders opposed the deal on the grounds of value: Leeds were to receive a total of £13.5m, while Sky was to get 9.1 per cent of the club's shares in addition to the rights agency. The deal valued Leeds at £101m at a time when its stock market valuation was £82.7m and critics felt that Sky should have paid more. Considering that when Sky did a similar deal with Chelsea, Sky's £40m investment valued the club at £404m, while the stock market valued Chelsea at £135m, they may have had a point. Sky paid nearly three times the market price for its share in Chelsea but only 1.22 times the market value for Leeds shares. In addition to questions over whether Sky had paid enough, there was also concern that the club was giving away too much in sacrificing 30 per cent of some media and sponsorship income. Although Sky's job was to find a buyer for rights, it could outbid its rivals by up to 30 per cent, knowing that it would recoup the premium in commission. Peter Ridsdale defends the deal to this day, pointing out that lucrative long-term sponsorship deals with Nike and Strongbow had already been signed and therefore fell outside of the terms of the Sky agency deal. Ridsdale also points out that the £13.5m enabled the club to strengthen the squad at a crucial time. Indeed, after the deal was announced Leeds bought four players – Huckerby, Wilcox, Hay and Milosovic – for a combined £7.3m. In retrospect the Leeds/BSkyB deal does look as if it has been a lot more worthwhile for the football club than for the broadcaster. Because Leeds qualified for the Champions League in 1999, the only commission that Sky has so far earned is for the TV rights to the four UEFA Cup rounds that Leeds played in the 2000–01 season.

Shortly after Sky had completed its deal with Leeds it signed a similar deal with Manchester City, paying £5.5m for a 9.9 per cent stake. NTL responded by negotiating a deal with Newcastle United that converted its stake, retained after it withdrew its bid for the club, into an agency agreement. Aston Villa, Middlesbrough and Leicester City were later added to the NTL stable, while Chelsea signed with Sky. Additionally, Liverpool and Arsenal signed deals with Granada that led to the formation of joint venture companies that would exploit media rights. The crucial differences between the Granada deals and those that Sky and NTL had with clubs was that the latter deals were for a fixed five-year term, while the Granada joint ventures were in perpetuity. However, all deals saw the media companies take a stake in a club and all deals saw the clubs receive a cash injection. When questioned at some length by the author on the benefits of Aston Villa's deal with NTL, Finance Director Mark Ansell wearily spelt out what he considered to be the main benefit: 'twenty-five million pounds'. While there has been much speculation as to why the media companies went to such trouble to obtain largely ineffectual stakes in a few English clubs, the motivation for the clubs is clear: money, and more of it than their rivals.

With both Football Association and Premier League multi-club ownership rules limiting any entity that owned shares in more than a single club to a maximum 10 per cent stake, it is questionable what level of control, if any, the media companies were able to exert over clubs when the time came to negotiate the Premier League TV deal in 2000. Perhaps the stakes should be looked at as another fall-back position. If Premier League rights were no longer sold collectively by the League, but on an individual basis by the clubs, then those media companies with stakes in clubs would obviously be in pole position. In the event, Sky and NTL both got what they wanted from the 2001–04 deal: Sky continued to hold the all-important 66-live-games-a-season rights, while NTL secured the pay-per-view rights, although it was later to withdraw its £328m offer and settle for a share in a consortium that paid £100m.

By June 2000 media companies had stakes in 11 English clubs. Granada had its joint ventures with Liverpool and Arsenal, BSkyB had stakes in Manchester United, Leeds United, Chelsea, Manchester City and Sunderland, while NTL had acquired stakes in Aston Villa, Newcastle United, Middlesbrough and Leicester City. In all cases the stakes held were less than the regulatory 10 per cent and, with the exception of Manchester United, involved a media agency agreement. That said, it is hard to see at this time exactly what the media companies have gained from their investments. In all cases the stakes are worth less on the market than was paid for them, the next Premier League TV deal will commence after the agency deals have expired and the TV rights that are available under the agency agreements remain for the UEFA and Intertoto Cups. However, the fact remains that the jostling for a place at the negotiating table for the 2001–04 Premier League TV rights introduced another element into the expanding ownership of English football.

There was yet another constituency that bought into the game during the late 1990s: the fans. Some clubs that joined the stock market explicitly targeted supporters with their share issues. Nottingham Forest, for example, offered shareholders a discount on season tickets, and most share issues enabled fans to buy shares in their clubs. The campaign against BSkyB's bid for Manchester United led to the formation of the Shareholders United group, which acts as a lobbying group for supporters' interests at the club, meeting regularly with senior management. The supporters' trust movement has gone from strength to strength since a group of Northampton Town supporters bought control of their bankrupt club in 1992. Under the umbrella of government-funded Supporters Direct, supporters' trusts now have seats on the boards of 26 British clubs. The supporters' trust movement will be discussed in greater detail in the final chapter but it is worth noting its rise here in the context of how the ownership of English clubs has changed. One of the main impediments to the movement has been the massive rise in the value of top-flight clubs, despite recent stock-market losses. This has meant that supporters have been unable to buy meaningful stakes in larger clubs and their most notable successes have been rescuing smaller clubs from bankruptcy.

As the nature of clubs has changed, so has the regulatory and competitive environment within which they operate. The most significant recent change in the competitive environment has been the formation of the Premier League in 1992, which has affected not only the clubs that have participated in it but also those that haven't. The increasing financial gap between Premiership clubs and those in the leagues below is one of the main reasons for the game's current crisis. The massive financial rewards that accrue from Premiership status have led clubs to spend excessively whether in attempting to join the Premiership or simply stay in it. The formation of the Premier League is probably one of the most important developments in the modern English game and therefore deserves a chapter in its own right.

## ENDNOTES

[1] Tottenham Hotspur. 27 October 1999. Preliminary results analysts' briefing.
[2] Russell, D. 1997. *Football and the English*. London: Carnegie.
[3] Conn, D. 1997. *The Football Business*. Edinburgh: Mainstream.
[4] Ibid.
[5] AFP, 29 May 2002.

# 3. Premiership

IN ORDER TO FULLY UNDERSTAND FOOTBALL'S CURRENT FINANCIAL CRISIS IT IS NECESSARY TO appreciate the context within which it is taking place. English football in the new millennium has been shaped by events at the close of the previous one, in particular the late 1980s and early 1990s. Firstly, the disasters at Bradford, Heysel and Hillsborough in 1985 and 1989 led to a massive programme of stadium building and renovation as the game implemented the 1991 Taylor Report. Secondly, the birth of pay television in the late 1980s introduced new competition to the television industry which led to inflation in the value of football television rights, which in turn led to a massive rise in clubs' and players' incomes. Thirdly, the foundation of the Premier League in 1992 radically changed the way that the money coming into the game was distributed, as well as creating another governing body to add to the FA and the Football League. Finally, the Bosman ruling of 1995 represented the greatest change in the relationship between players and clubs since the abolition of the maximum wage in 1960.

The formation of the Premier League in 1992 heralded a revolution in English professional football. While the Bosman ruling of 1995 and the three television contracts signed since the Premier League was formed have all had a major effect on the economics of English football, the foundation of the Premier League produced a new paradigm within which these events took place. The formation of the Premier League was not just about the economics of football but also about its politics. The economic dynamics that led to the creation of the Premier League have always been present in English football: large clubs wanting a larger share of the money generated by the game. However, the formation of the Premier League occurred when it did because of the political climate within English football at the time. The long-running power struggle between the Football League and the Football Association had its roots in the dispute over professionalism in the 1880s and manifested itself in disputes over all aspects of the game, from the FA's attempt to impose a maximum transfer fee in 1905 to its instruction to League clubs over the payment of expenses to amateur players in 1965.

Even though it was sanctioned by the FA, the Premier League was, and remains, a breakaway league, in exactly the same way as the proposed European Superleague plan of 1998 and the recent Phoenix League were. The driving principle behind the formation of a breakaway league is the desire of those who breakaway to keep more of the money that an existing league produces. In the 1980s the so-called Big Five of Liverpool, Manchester United, Everton, Tottenham and Arsenal felt that as they were the most popular clubs they therefore generated the most revenue. They argued, therefore, that it was only fair that they received a larger slice of the League's income. In 1983 the first steps towards a breakaway were taken when it was agreed that clubs would keep all the gate money generated at home games, instead of sharing it with the visitors. Another important step was taken in 1985 when the League's voting structure was changed so that decisions regarding the distribution of TV and sponsorship money only required a two-third, rather than a three-quarters majority. It was in 1986 that the biggest concessions were wrung out of the League by the big clubs. First Division clubs were now allocated 50 per cent of future television and sponsorship income, 25 per cent was allocated to the Second Division, with the Third and Fourth sharing the remaining 25 per cent. A new TV deal with ITV helped to mitigate the damage to the lower-division clubs in the short term, but the long-term effect was a widening of the gap between the large and small clubs. This is a very important point that it is worth emphasising. When in 1998, the Scottish Premier League was formed as a breakaway from the Scottish Football League, it was able to do so with the League's consent because the breakaway league was able to compensate those left behind with some of the proceeds of a greatly enhanced TV deal. When there was talk in 1999 of an Atlantic League, whereby Glasgow Rangers and Celtic were proposing to leave the SPL and join a European league, the SPL Chief Executive Roger Mitchell said that the remaining clubs would accept the move as they would be paid compensation. While these pay-offs may help in the short term, it is the differential between clubs that becomes the issue in the long term. This is one of the fundamentals of the peculiar economics of football, or any professional team sport where there is a market for players. The disparity between clubs' spending power in the player market is at the heart of the game's current financial crisis. As clubs invest for success, the richest clubs gradually push up the prices that the best players can command. There is then a trickle-down effect, where values are increased throughout the player market. A smaller club that has sold a player to a larger club then spends the proceeds on a cheaper replacement and is able to outbid its rivals. The inflation in player wages and transfer fees is led from the top, by the big clubs competing with each other for the best players; inflation then spreads throughout the game. As the better players become too expensive for the middling and smaller clubs, these clubs have to extend themselves further in order to compete. The actual sums involved are irrelevant; it is the differences in income and spending power that are important.

Very often it is the threat of breakaway that is sufficient for the larger clubs to achieve some of the aims. This was the case in 1985, when the threatened breakaway was averted by the granting of the concessions mentioned above. Similarly, in 1998, the threat of the European Superleague, as proposed by the Italian agency Media Partners, managed to force UEFA into a complete reformatting of European club competition with the introduction of group stages in the Champions League. Europe's larger clubs, later to form the lobbying group G14, thus achieved a *de facto* superleague by threatening to go it alone. In 1992, however, the League felt that no more concessions could be granted and, crucially, the breakaway clubs, aware of developments in the broadcast market that would deliver even more money, wanted more than just concessions.

It could be said that in many ways the Football League contributed to the formation of the Premier League by taking on the Football Association over the issue of the size of the First Division. In August 1990 the League voted for a return to a 22-club top flight. Apart from other issues, the increase would give the clubs another four more games and around ten per cent in extra gate money. There was also a certain degree of antagonism towards the so-called Big Five over the number of times they were featured on ITV and who were in favour of a smaller First Division. However, the staunchest opponent of a return to a 22-club First Division was the Football Association. Although the FA consistently argued that a smaller top flight was in the best interests of the England team because it would leave players fresher for internationals, another less-cited reason for its opposition to an expanded top flight was financial. As now, the FA's main sources of revenue were the FA Cup and England internationals, be they competitive or friendlies. A 22-club First Division would increase fixture congestion leaving less space for the FA's fixtures. Recently the demands of European competition have increased the big clubs' interest in reducing the size of the Premier League, but that was less of a factor in the early 1990s. In *The Guardian* on 3 August 1992 League president Bill Fox casually dismissed the FA's objection by pointing out that England won the 1966 World Cup with a 22-club First Division, but, in the same article, Chief Executive Arthur Sandford pointed to another reason behind the expansion: 'But we have to face up to the bill facing football for the Taylor Report and this was one factor in the decision. In the First Division a tremendous amount of work will have to be done if it is to go all-seater within five years.' Fox also explained that the League wanted more power: 'We have got to have a greater say in what goes on in the national association. We were looking towards changing the workings of the FA. We have several members on the FA council. But it is not in the interests of some council members to go along this route.'

There has been much written about the birth of the Premiership, much of it concentrating on the personalities involved. In his classic text on the football business, David Conn concentrates on the role of a number of club chairmen, in particular Tottenham Hotspur's Sir Alan Sugar and Arsenal's David Dein. Alex Fynn and Anthony King both identify Crystal Palace's Ron Noades and Chelsea's Ken Bates, the so called Bates/Noades axis, as crucial in getting a sufficient number of smaller clubs behind the idea of a breakaway from the Football League. While the clubs that formed the original Premier League were obviously the main drivers of the breakaway, the Football Association also played a crucial role. Indeed without the support of the Football Association, any breakaway would have been dead in the water as the Association is the game's ultimate authority in England. While it may have been feasible for the clubs to breakaway without the consent of the FA, it would have meant them being ineligible for European competition and could even have meant that their players would have been prohibited from representing their countries in international competition.

There was a common consensus within football in 1990 that the game was in crisis. The disasters at Bradford, Heysel and Hillsborough had led to two inquiries and reports and the government was taking an interest in the public-order issues raised by hooliganism. The continuing friction between the Football Association and the League was identified as one of the problems and it was the League that rose to the challenge first. The publication of the Football League report *One Game, One Team, One Voice* in October 1990 was an attempt to overcome the historic divide between the two governing bodies. The central proposal of *One Game* was the formation of a joint board of 12 members to run the game – six members drawn from the League and six from the FA. The Football Association did not see *One Game* as an attempt to build bridges but more as an attempt by the League to gain power. League Chairman Bill Fox lobbied the FA's 92 councillors throughout the summer of 1990, knowing he would in effect be asking them to vote like turkeys for Christmas, but it was felt by the League that the FA would be reassured by the 50 per cent representation on the new board. As Fynn and Conn both point out, however, it was not the part-time FA councillors that provided the toughest opposition to the League's proposals for reform but the career administrators at the Association, in particular the FA's Chief Executive Graham Kelly. Kelly's response to *One Game* was his own document called *A Blueprint for the Future of Football*.

The central argument of the *Blueprint* was that the setting up of an 18-club Premier League would benefit the English national team:

> For the game to prosper in England, we need a successful England Team. To have a successful England Team, we need the fullest support of the Football League, which means the Football League should occupy a subordinate position to that of the England Team in the pyramid of playing excellence. In order to elevate the England Team to the apex of playing excellence there are two basic requirements:
>
> A smaller First Division (18 clubs)
> A unified approach[1]

As we shall see, the *Blueprint* created neither a smaller First Division nor a unified approach. Had it done so, it is arguable whether it would have led to a more successful England team. That it didn't, and that the England team has not improved, is beyond doubt.

The *Blueprint* makes several references to the conflict between the FA and the League and states on many occasions that the only way it could be resolved is for the 'League to be subordinate to the Football Association'. The League's proposal to end the power struggle through a power-sharing agreement 'has been rejected by the Football Association Council, and properly so'.

In order to head off a challenge from the League, Kelly basically adopted a strategy of divide and rule. The Football League was divided, between the large and small clubs, and Kelly proposed that the FA rule over the larger clubs which broke away to form the Premier League. In his book *The Football Business* David Conn quotes Kelly's account of how the potential breakaway clubs' plans coincided with those of the FA: 'David Dein [Arsenal Chief Executive] and Noel White [Liverpool Chairman] approached us about breaking away from the Football League and it coincided with what we were doing.'[2]

With the previously conservative Liverpool joining Arsenal, Tottenham and Manchester United in the breakaway movement and the FA putting its weight behind the idea, the Premier League concept began to gather momentum. The same FA council meeting that had rejected the League's power-sharing proposals also overruled the League's changes to its regulations that required clubs to give three years notice if they intended to resign. That regulation was imposed specifically to impede the formation of a breakaway and although the League challenged the FA's ruling in the high court in July 1991, it failed and the final constitutional impediment to the formation of the Premier League was overcome.

Although the legal position was clear and the way open for the League's formation, it still required a membership beyond the so-called Big Five of Arsenal, Liverpool, Manchester United, Everton and Tottenham Hotspur. Here the role of Chelsea and Crystal Palace chairmen Ken Bates and Ron Noades proved crucial to the future shape of the Premier League. Bates and Noades offered their support and the support of other smaller First Division clubs on the condition that the Premiership would consist of 22 clubs, to be reduced to 20 by 1994, and that each member club would have one vote. The demand for 22 clubs seriously undermined the FA's reason for supporting the breakaway but it became the price that the FA had to pay in order to secure the support of the majority of First Division clubs. The Bates/Noades argument was that the revenues generated by 22 clubs were necessary for the clubs to improve their stadia to be compliant with the Taylor Report by 1994. Arsenal's David Dein managed to negotiate a reduction to 20 by 1994. Before the start of the 1991–92 season the entire First Division gave one years' notice to quit the Football League. The Premier League was born.

The Premier League that kicked off on 15 August 1992 was very different from the one that had been envisaged in the FA's *Blueprint*. Not only was it larger, it was effectively autonomous from the FA and the Football League. The *Blueprint*'s central purpose was to consolidate the FA's position as the single governing body in the game, but instead it created a third, stronger, force that would eventually become more powerful than the Football League which the FA had been trying to supplant.

At first glance the Premier League's political structure appears to follow the model of the Football League. Each member club has one vote and a two-thirds majority is required for major decisions. This means that as few as six clubs can veto any proposals and that at least 14 must agree to change. This mechanism works well to stop the larger clubs dictating the Premiership's agenda, but it also means that any reforms that would favour smaller clubs are unlikely to succeed. In 2000, for example, Coventry proposed a change in the way that television money was distributed. The money had previously been split three ways: 50 per cent was distributed equally among the 20 clubs; 25 per cent was awarded to clubs according to their final league placing (called the merit award); and the remaining 25 per cent was awarded according to the number of times each club's matches were televised (known as the facility fee). Although there was a guarantee that each club would be featured on television at least once, it has unsurprisingly become the case that the larger clubs have been featured more often than the smaller ones. This has led to a further polarisation of wealth towards the larger clubs, which is what Coventry attempted to address with its proposal. The Coventry resolution sought to do away with the facility fee and add the 25 per cent to money shared equally. The proposal was popular with many clubs and many predicted that it would receive the requisite 14 votes. However, the proposal only received 12 votes, with 8 clubs voting against and it was later reported that

West Ham and Derby County voted with the larger clubs, while all other clubs voted according to how many times they were usually featured on television. Neither club has ever commented publicly on their perverse voting so it can only be speculated that they either believed they would be better off with the status quo or that they were worried that the larger clubs would resign from the Premiership and set up an alternative breakaway league if the proposal was successful.

The Premier League is different to both the FA and the Football League in that it does not have a board of directors or any standing committees. The executive functions of the League are carried out by its independent chairman, chief executive and commercial director, who are appointed by all the clubs. This means that clubs are actually more powerful than their Football League counterparts and FA councillors as both the other bodies have boards and standing committees, which have considerable power. It was this aspect of the Premiership that was particularly attractive to the member club chairmen as they were now truly masters of their own destiny. There is more than a little irony, however, in that the balance of power within the Premiership now resided with the majority of clubs rather than the Big Five who had originally instigated the breakaway.

Theoretically, the Premiership's executive is answerable to the member clubs and the relationship between the first chief executive Rick Parry and the clubs appeared to be a reasonably healthy one. Parry played a crucial role in the formation of the Premiership and negotiated the League's first two television deals, both of which comfortably exceeded most chairmen's expectations. Parry left the post in 1997 to become chief executive of the club he supported, Liverpool, and was replaced by the lawyer and former Tottenham director Peter Leaver.

Although Leaver was an experienced QC, he had little knowledge of the value of television rights and was ill-equipped to deal with the complexities presented by the advent of digital and cable platforms. It soon became apparent that the next television deal would be very different from the 1992 and 1996 deals, not least because of concerns expressed by both the Office of Fair Trading and the European Commission over the length and terms of those deals. Leaver decided that he would seek some expert advice in the shape of former BSkyB executives Sam Chisholm and David Chance. Leaver agreed to pay the consultants fees of around £650,000 per year each, with the possibility of them earning an additional £50m if the next deal was worth more than £1bn. Understandably, the chairmen were furious at the size of the fees, and also angry that Leaver refused to divulge the sums at first, citing confidentiality agreements with the consultants. Leaver's legal background ultimately led to his downfall as he was asked by the chairmen not to pay the two any money, but he did so, fearing they would have a case against the Premiership for breach of contract. That added to the chairmen's anger because they were unaware that any contract was in place and Leaver was sacked, receiving £300,000 in compensation.

The Leaver, Chisholm and Chance saga illustrated the madness at the height of football's boom. Although the 2000 television deal would indeed prove complex, was it complex to the tune of £50m? The idea that two individuals could justifiably earn such sums advising the Premier League on the sale of TV rights caused consternation throughout the game and raised questions about the concept of the Premier League's executive independence. Leaver took that concept to an extreme, not only acting independently of the chairmen, but actually going against their stated wishes. After Leaver was sacked, the Premiership may have wondered about going back to the concept of a committee of chairmen to negotiate deals, but instead chose to replace Leaver, and Sir John Quinton – the Premier League's Chairman since its inception – with former Football League Chief Executive Richard Scudamore and former Sheffield Wednesday Chairman David Richards. The choice of Richards raised some eyebrows among observers as his club were on the verge of relegation and would go down to the First Division with at least £16m of debt. However, he was popular among fellow chairmen and, unlike Leaver, could be trusted not to act against their wishes.

At the time the FA justified its support of the Premier League as a way of improving the quality of English football, which in turn was meant to improve the quality of the English team itself. The FA's chief executive at the time was Graham Kelly and he put it thus: 'The proposed new structure, with appropriate arrangements for the sharing of revenues, will benefit the national team and the national game as a whole.'[3] While few took this justification seriously, preferring instead to point to the ongoing power struggle between the FA and the Football League, the absence of a subsequent retrospective explanation means that it will have to suffice. As England had reached the semi-finals of the 1990 World Cup, it would take a World Cup final appearance by England to justify the FA's 1991 position.

By the FA's own standards therefore, with England's failure to even qualify for USA '94 and then to be eliminated in a quarter-final in France four years later, the Premier League has failed to deliver. Victory in Japan and Korea in 2002 would have called that verdict into question, but anything less, when compared to England's record in the ten years preceding the breakaway (1982 reached second round; 1986 quarter-finals; 1990 semi-finals) would mean that, after ten years, the Premier League cannot in any way be shown to have improved the quality of the England team. That is an objective statistical fact, not a matter of mere subjective sporting opinion. It is interesting to note that in the aftermath of England's quarter-final elimination from the 2002 World Cup by Brazil, Coach Sven-Goran Eriksson called for a reduction in the size of the Premier League. Eriksson blamed the demands of the domestic season for tiring his players but the chances of the Premier League voting for fewer fixtures, and less money, remain as slim as ever. In fact, with the increasing wealth gap between the Premier League and the First Division it is even less likely that any Premiership club would vote for anything that would increase their chances of relegation.

The question as to whether the formation of the Premiership has benefited the national game as a whole is more likely to elicit a subjective answer. Whether or not the football so copiously displayed on various free-to-air, subscription and pay-per-view channels now is of a better quality than that shown on ITV's *The Big Match* over ten years ago would be the ideal subject for pub pundits to argue about contentiously and probably cannot be answered definitively. Those who argue that it is, will undoubtedly point to the presence of a plethora of foreign stars currently plying their trade in the Premiership. It could be argued, however, that these players would have come anyway because the Bosman ruling made it much easier for players to move between clubs and even countries. It is interesting to note that the influx significantly increased after 1995 and it would seem their presence cannot be ascribed solely to the existence of the Premier League. A more compelling argument that the Premier League has enhanced the quality of the English game appears to be the record of English clubs in European competition.

Analysis of the performance of English clubs in Europe prior to the formation of the Premier League is complicated by the five-year ban imposed by UEFA on English clubs participating in Europe following the

Heysel tragedy in 1985. English clubs were readmitted in 1990 and Manchester United promptly won the 1990 Cup-Winners' Cup. Arsenal represented England as champions the following year, but were eliminated by Benfica in the second round of the Champions Cup. It could be argued that the results of English clubs in Europe in the two years before the formation of the Premiership were distorted by the effects of the ban and also by the fact that England did not have a competitor in the Champions Cup of 1990. In order to reach a judgment on the effect of the Premiership on English clubs' performance in European competition, it is probably fairer to compare the ten years prior to the 1985 ban with the ten years following the formation of the Premier League. In the ten years prior to the post-Heysel ban English clubs won seven Champions Cup finals and were losing finalists twice. The Cup-Winners' Cup was less fruitful with Everton's victory in 1985 the only success, and Arsenal's losing 1980 final appearance was the only other occasion when an English club reached the final. The UEFA Cup provided two English champions in Tottenham and Ipswich but no losing finalists, so out of thirty European finals in the ten years prior to the ban, English clubs won ten of them and were beaten finalists on three occasions. Analysis of the ten years following the formation of the Premier League is complicated by the merging of the UEFA Cup and Cup-Winners' Cup in 1999, which leaves just twenty-seven European finals of which English clubs have won four and lost two. There are of course a number of other variables that impact on the success of English teams. The expansion of UEFA following the collapse of the Berlin Wall in 1989, to the point whereby there are now 52 member federations, means that in some respects it is harder to succeed because of increased competition. However, UEFA's system of coefficients means that the success of a country's clubs is rewarded by awarding more places to that country. With more teams entered success should be easier to come by. Given these variables, it is probably impossible to say definitively that English clubs have fared worse in Europe because of the formation of the Premier League, but it is surely equally impossible to say that the standard of English clubs has significantly improved in relation to those of other European countries. The fact remains that during the ten years prior to the formation of the Premier League, English clubs dominated the Champions Cup (winning seven times) and occasionally won the lesser competitions (three times), yet since its formation English clubs have won the

Champions League just once and the lesser competitions three times.

Of the 22 clubs that started the first Premier League season in 1992, only nine of them will start the eleventh, and of that nine, only eight – Arsenal, Manchester United, Liverpool, Chelsea, Aston Villa, Tottenham Hotspur, Southampton and Everton – have been constant participants over the last ten years. As well as the League reducing in size to 20 clubs the elitist nature of the division appears to have been cemented of late, as while 22 different clubs have been relegated, only 19 different clubs have been promoted. Over the first ten years of existence, the League has given rise to a number of yo-yo clubs. Nottingham Forest and Crystal Palace share the dubious honour of being relegated the most, each dropping down three times. Five clubs – Leicester City, Ipswich Town, Middlesbrough, Manchester City and Bolton – have been relegated twice.

While relegation from the Premiership still represents the biggest threat to a club's finances, there would appear to be little correlation between the number of times relegated and financial health. True, Palace and Forest have both had serious financial problems with the former going into administration and the latter suspending its shares on the Alternative Investment Market, but the clubs twice relegated appear, at the time of writing, to have survived the experience relatively unscathed.

The phenomenon known as the 'yo-yo effect', whereby clubs frequently move between the top two divisions, has become more pronounced since the formation of the Premier League. Research carried out in 2000 by Patrick Murphy of the University of Leicester analysed promotion and relegation since the end of the Second World War.[4] Incidences whereby clubs were relegated one season and promoted the following season, and vice versa (called sequential movements), have increased dramatically during the period. For example, between 1950 and 1960 there were thirteen sequential movements, the following decade there were nine. Between 1970 and 1980 there were eighteen and between 1980 and 1990 there were twenty-one. However, in the decade from 1992 to 2002, that is the first ten seasons of the Premier League, there were thirty-three sequential movements between the top two divisions. While it could be argued that there has been a gradual increase in the yo-yo phenomenon since the Second World War, it is obvious that the trend has been exacerbated since the formation of the Premiership. The yo-yo phenomenon is an indicator that it is becoming increasingly difficult for clubs promoted to the Premier League to establish themselves in it, while at the same time it is becoming easier for clubs relegated to the First Division to secure promotion back to the Premiership. The reasons for this are quite obvious; clubs joining the Premiership immediately face a short-fall in resources compared to their competitors, while those relegated enjoy an advantage over theirs. Usually, as well as joining the First Division with a stronger and more expensive playing squad, clubs relegated from the Premier League are paid a 'parachute' payment – a percentage of television revenue to soften the blow. After the latest television deal, the parachute payment, as 50 per cent of the equal share, was £3.9m. That is more than any First Division club could have expected to earn from the ITV Digital deal and represents a significant advantage for a relegated club over its competitors. That said, it still only offers minimal compensation for the loss of Premier League income. The parachute payment of £3.9m received in August 2000 by six First Division clubs that had been promoted in the previous two years is still a long way short of the £10.8m that Leicester received as the Premier League's bottom club.

It could be argued that the yo-yo effect has actually been beneficial to the English game as it has contributed to a steady turnover of clubs in the top flight. In the 10 years prior to the formation of the Premier League 38 different clubs played in the First Division while in the 10-year history of the Premier League there have been 35. It would be wrong to draw any firm conclusions from such a small difference and it is not possible to ascertain whether the reduction is part of a historical trend as a comparative analysis of previous decades is not possible because only two clubs were relegated prior to 1974. Nevertheless, the fact remains that clubs are finding it increasingly difficult to stay in the Premier League after gaining promotion from the First Division.

There are several ways that the wealth gap between the Premier League and the First Division could be bridged. The most obvious would be to increase the parachute payment to relegated clubs. This was in fact proposed at the Premier League's 2002 summer meeting as a one-off payment to mitigate against the consequences of the ITV Digital collapse, but was unsurprisingly rejected. A consequence of increasing the parachute payment would be to increase the financial advantage that relegated clubs enjoy over the rest of the First Division, which in turn would lead to more yo-yo clubs at the expense of clubs rising through the

**Table 3.1: Premier League Promotion and Relegation**

| | 92–93 | 93–94 | 94–95 | 95–96 | 96–97 | 97–98 | 98–99 | 99–00 | 00–01 | 01–02 |
|---|---|---|---|---|---|---|---|---|---|---|
| Barnsley | | | | | P | R | | | | |
| Birmingham | | | | | | | | | | P |
| Blackburn | | | | | | | R | | P | |
| Bolton | | | P | R | P | R | | | P | |
| Bradford | | | | | | | P | | R | |
| Charlton | | | | | | P | R | P | | |
| Coventry | | | | | | | | | R | |
| Crystal Palace | R | P | R | | P | R | | | | |
| Derby | | | | P | | | | | | R |
| Fulham | | | | | | | | | P | |
| Ipswich | | | R | | | | | P | | R |
| Leicester | | P | R | P | | | | | | R |
| Man City | | | | R | | | | P | R | P |
| Middlesbro | R | | P | | R | P | | | | |
| Newcastle | P | | | | | | | | | |
| Norwich | | | R | | | | | | | |
| N. Forest | R | P | | | R | P | R | | | |
| Oldham | | R | | | | | | | | |
| QPR | | | | R | | | | | | |
| Sheff U | | R | | | | | | | | |
| Sheff W | | | | | | | | R | | |
| Sunderland | | | | P | R | | P | | | |
| Swindon | P | R | | | | | | | | |
| Watford | | | | | | | P | R | | |
| WBA | | | | | | | | | | P |
| West Ham | P | | | | | | | | | |
| Wimbledon | | | | | | | | R | | |

*Source: Patrick Murphy and Angela Breckenridge*

divisions. An alternative could be for the money that the Premiership currently pays in parachute payments to be paid to all 24 First Division clubs. That would amount to around £1m for each club but its effect on the income gap would be negligible. It would also be even more unlikely than the proposal for increasing the parachute payment to receive the support of the sufficient number of Premier League clubs. Premier League clubs tolerate the current level of parachute payments simply because they know that they could one day be the grateful recipients of them; on that basis they could hardly be expected to vote for a proposal to reduce them. Because the Premier League only exists to further the interests of members, it is never going to address the problems caused by the wealth gap for the rest of football. The responsibility for bridging the gap therefore lies firmly with the Football League. Hence the First Division's enthusiasm for the idea of a Phoenix League incorporating the Old Firm clubs – seen as a way that the First Division could command additional television revenue and gate money and go some way towards bridging the gap. Although the wealth gap has been caused by the creation of the Premiership, the responsibility for bridging it lies firmly with the Football League.

The Premier League may have failed to do for English football what the FA expected it to, but in its own terms it has been an unmitigated success. Premier League attendances have grown year on year and the Taylor-compliant stadia are usually filled to near capacity. Such has been its success in selling its television rights that the Premiership is able to attract some of the world's best talent. The Premiership is viewed by over 500 million people in 130 countries as a result of the £85m overseas television deal with a consortium that includes News Corp, Sport+ and Octagon CSI/TWI, which has helped the Premier League build support all over the world. However, the Premier League success story has occurred at a time when football TV rights have been rising worldwide. The real test will come when those values start to fall, as they surely will. There is a belief in the Premier League that although the value of domestic television rights may fall, the value of overseas rights will continue to rise. That may well be the case but will they rise by more than the fall in domestic rights? That is a crucial question that is unanswerable at present.

Although the Premier League may not appear to be in crisis at present, its future is under threat on a number of fronts. Not only is the value of television rights uncertain, but also is the Premier League's ability to sell them collectively. The big clubs want more control over their rights and the decision to allow clubs access to delayed highlights for broadcast on their own television channels or websites is possibly the thin edge of a large wedge. Another worry for the Premier League is the European Commission's interest in the way that it sells TV rights. The Commission has been keeping a watchful eye on the way that both UEFA and the Premier League sell their TV rights to make sure that deals do not limit consumer choice or competition between broadcasters. Like the Office of Fair Trading in 1999, the Commission is concerned that exclusive deals with broadcasters are uncompetitive and the Premier League has been careful to construct its deals in such a way that allows different broadcasters a slice of the action. The current Premier League TV deal, for example, gives Sky live games, ITV highlights and a consortium of broadcasters the live pay-per-view matches. The length of the current deal is for four years but UEFA has limited its next Champions League deal to two years to keep the Commission happy and it would be no surprise if the next Premiership deal was for three or even two years only. While that may well foster competition between broadcasters, it could prove problematic for clubs that have signed players on four- or five-year contracts.

The biggest threat to the future of the Premier League will come from its member clubs and their ability to remain solvent throughout the current crisis. The inflationary pressures of the Premiership have lead to massive debt levels for some of its member clubs (see Chapter 5). Should the Premier League fail to deliver sufficient income for those clubs to be able to service those debts, financial meltdown at the top of the English game will surely follow.

## ENDNOTES

[1]  The Football Association. 1991. A *Blueprint for the Future of Football*: 38.
[2]  Conn, D. 1997. *The Football Business*. Edinburgh: Mainstream: 147.
[3]  Ibid.
[4]  Murphy, P. 1998–99 Season. 'Banking on Success: Examining the Links Between Performance and the Increasing Concentration of Wealth in English Elite Football', in *Singer & Friedlander Football Review*.

# 4. Relegation

THE CREATION OF THE PREMIER LEAGUE IN 1992 FUNDAMENTALLY CHANGED THE ECONOMICS of English football. The increased income that it generated introduced an opportunity for those clubs that play in it to compete more successfully with their counterparts in Europe. It has raised the profile of the English game internationally with over 500 million people watching the Premier League each week in 130 countries. But it has also introduced a new hazard that clubs have become desperate to avoid: relegation. Obviously, relegation and promotion existed before the formation of the Premier League, but since its formation, the consequences of relegation have become more and more serious.

The Premier League's success has been to the detriment of the Football League because it has taken an ever-increasing proportion of football's total income. In the 1994–95 season, the Premier League clubs had a combined income of £323m compared to £146m for the 72 clubs of the Football League. The following year, the last of the original BSkyB television contract, Premier League income had risen to £346m, while Football League income increased to £171m. The gap between the two had widened, but only by £2m and as a proportion of total revenue the Football League's share had risen from 31 per cent to 33 per cent. The next season, however, saw the gap widen dramatically as the new £670m BSkyB deal kicked in; the Premier League's income for 1996–97 was £464m, an increase of 34 per cent, while Football League income rose by just 24 per cent to £211m. The Premier League was now earning 31 per cent of total income again but over the next four seasons that proportion dropped to 28 per cent so by the 1999–2000 season the Premier League had income of £772m and the Football League

£305m. English football had broken through the £1bn barrier; within two years the Premier League would do so on its own.

On a general level, the increase in the income gap between the Premiership and the Football League is dramatic, but when looked at specifically in terms of individual clubs the effect of the gap on clubs is startling. Of the 20 different clubs that have suffered relegation from the Premier League, four – Bradford, Crystal Palace, Queens Park Rangers and Swindon Town – have subsequently gone into administration. Of the 16 others, Nottingham Forest have had to have their shares suspended as they were unable to file their accounts; Norwich and Sheffield United have recently had to appeal to supporters to raise funds; Leicester City and Watford have had to cut their staff numbers; Sheffield Wednesday and Coventry have debts of £16m and £60m respectively; while Derby County are looking for new investors as they struggle under £27m of debt. Wimbledon, of course, have been forced, according to the owners, to move to Milton Keynes or face liquidation. That leaves seven clubs who are in reasonable financial health, of which all bar Ipswich have returned to the Premier League.

In 1997 Bolton Wanderers were promoted from the First Division to the Premiership and saw their turnover increase by 105 per cent, from £7.65m to £15.7m. Similarly, when Bradford City achieved promotion to the Premiership in 2000, turnover leapt by 170 per cent, from £7.8m to £21m. Thanks to the existence of the parachute payment that compensates clubs relegated from the Premiership by paying them a proportion of television income for two years after relegation, the effect of relegation at first looks to be less marked than that of promotion. Blackburn Rovers were relegated from the Premiership in 2000 and suffered a 39 per cent fall in income to £12.88m from £21.27m, while Nottingham Forest experienced a 44 per cent fall in turnover from £17.51m to £9.48m. However, turnover is only half the story as clubs usually invest in their playing squads once promotion to the Premiership has been achieved and their wage bills increase as a consequence. Take the case of the two clubs above; Blackburn had been relegated after seven seasons in the top flight and took a wage bill of £22.11m down with them. With a turnover of only £12.88m it is no surprise that Rovers made an operating loss of £15.76m, which brought the club's debts to a massive £70m. Rovers were comfortable with their debt as they had the backing of Sir Jack Walker, the multi-millionaire tax exile who bankrolled the club throughout the 1990s and financed the club's victorious Premiership campaign of 1994–95. With Sir Jack behind them, money was no object for Rovers.

Nottingham Forest also carried on the burden of a Premier League wage bill after they were relegated to the First Division in 1999, one that cost £10.9m in the 1999–2000 season. With a turnover of just £9.48m the wage bill helped Forest report an operating loss of £5.66m, taking the club's debts to £10.1m. That debt level was the beginning of the end for Forest. Two years later Forest were on the verge of bankruptcy and their shares on the Alternative Investment Market were suspended after the club was unable to file their accounts. How Forest arrived at that situation is an object lesson in how *not* to deal with relegation. As well as poor financial management, Forest have also suffered from an acrimonious takeover battle, a subsequent long-running court case and a shambolic stock-market flotation. Hardly an ideal background against which to plot a successful strategy for surviving relegation from the Premier League.

Nottingham Forest share with Crystal Palace the dubious distinction of being relegated from the Premier League more than any other club. In the ten seasons since the formation of the Premier League, Forest have spent five in the Premiership and five in the First Division. Of those five seasons in the First Division, the club has had the benefit of the parachute payment for four of them so theoretically should have been better placed than most First Division clubs to survive financially. However, an extended three-season spell in the First Division since 1999 has seen the club suspend its shares and head towards administration.

Nottingham Forest is certainly a strong football brand. The personality of Brian Clough ensured that when the club was at the pinnacle of their success in the late 1970s, winning two European Champions Cups, the world knew all about it. Forest's success in Europe meant that the club became known internationally.

When Forest were relegated from the Premiership at the end of the competition's inaugural season, it followed a 16-season spell in the top flight. The club bounced straight back the following season and then enjoyed a highly successful 1994–95 season, finishing third and qualifying for the UEFA Cup. The resurgence only lasted for another season and Forest were relegated at the end of the 1996–97 season, after finishing bottom of the table. Financially, Forest's three seasons in the Premiership left the club in a parlous state. Turnover had risen from £10.29m in 1995 to £14.43m in 1997, but at the same time player wages had almost doubled from £4.9m to £8.3m, and although the club made a small pre-tax profit in 1995, they made a loss of £1.48m in 1997 and re-entered the First Division with £15.7m of debt.

Then Chairman Fred Reacher knew that investment was required and held meetings with Grant Bovey, an entrepreneur better known for his relationship with the media celebrity Anthea Turner. Bovey promised to invest £10m, but one of the barriers to investment in Forest was its anachronistic ownership structure, by which 209 shareholders held one £1 share each. The shares were not transferable and if any shareholders wanted to sell, they could only be sold back the club for £1. Furthermore, nobody could own more than one share. Bovey offered shareholders £24,000 each to change the club's constitution and transfer their shares to him, a move which required 75 per cent of shareholders to vote in favour.

Bovey recruited Anthea Turner to appear in a video circulated to shareholders, explaining his plans and outlining his offer, which promised an immediate investment of £25m into the club. Newspapers, however, discovered that Bovey's company, Watershed Pictures, was insolvent so Reacher started to look for other investors, placing an advertisement in the *Financial Times* offering: 'A unique opportunity for investors to assist the club in implementing its plans for the next millennium.'

The advert flushed out two rival consortiums, one headed by Sandy Anderson, who had amassed a personal fortune of £36m by selling the privatised rolling-stock leasing company Porterbrook to South West Trains. Anderson was joined by Nigel Doughty of the Doughty Hanson venture capital company, Charlie Scott, Chairman of the Cordiant advertising group, and two others. The Anderson consortium immediately offered to invest between £10m and £15m, with the prospect of a flotation three to five years down the line. The opposing consortium was led by Lawrie Lewis, chairman of the global exhibitions group Blenheim, former Tottenham Hotspur Chief Executive Irving Scholar and the writer and publisher Phil Soar. Like Bovey, the Lewis group offered shareholders £12,000 each and promised to invest £10m, followed by an immediate flotation. Lewis was the financial backer and said: 'I can write a cheque for £10m and it will clear. The Forest board have confirmation of that from my bankers.'[1] But before a bid was due to be presented to the board, Lewis inexplicably withdrew, leaving Scholar and Soar looking for new investors.

At first it looked as if Albert Scardino, husband of *Financial Times* publisher Pearson's Chief Executive Marjorie, with the backing of Mercury Asset Management and Electra Investments, would provide £20m for the consortium. Then Grant Bovey briefly resurfaced before Nigel Wray entered the fray. Wray made his fortune by floating Carlton Communications and then through the property company Burford Group. He was also the owner of Rugby Union club Saracens and had a growing reputation in the City.

The rival bids were put to shareholders on 6 January 1997 and in a letter circulated to shareholders that morning Phil Soar said: 'Many of you have said to me that what the club would really like is a Jack Walker. What we intend to offer you is not one but two Jack Walkers.' He then quoted the *Mail on Sunday* from 5 January 1997 which compared Wray to Jack Walker and Newcastle's Sir John Hall. He neglected to say which of Scardino and Scholar was the other Walker but he did implore shareholders to approach the meeting slowly in their cars as 'we don't want a prospective Jack Walker run over'.[2]

Eventually Forest shareholders voted for the Scholar/Wray and Soar bid (Scardino had withdrawn only to resurface some years later as the 'saviour' of Notts County), having been promised a cash injection of £11m for the club and a payment of £13,546 to each shareholder, or an equivalent shareholding in the new company which would be floated on the stock market as soon as possible.

The new owners immediately invested £8.8m in the playing squad, buying eight players, including Pierre van Hooijdonk and Marco Pascolo, and selling seven for a total of £3.8m. Van Hooijdonk quickly became disillusioned with the club and manager David Platt, describing the club as 'terribly amateurish', and he refused to play for several months before being sold two years later for £3.5m.

When Forest joined the Alternative Investment Market in October 1997 they were the seventeenth English club to join the stock market. The City, therefore, had plenty of experience of football club flotations and, despite the presence of Wray and fellow property developer Nick Leslau, who were held in high regard in the City, was hardly enthused by the prospect of a recently relegated club. It could be argued that had the float not been delayed by the takeover battle, it would have been more successful. In the event only £3m was raised after expenses, less than any of the other 1997 floats. The prospectus for the flotation stated that the club's first priority was to gain promotion back to the Premiership as soon as possible and that objective was achieved with Forest winning the First Division Championship. Promotion back to the Premiership saw income leap by 51 per cent to £17m, but wages were held at First Division levels, rising just 6 per cent to £11.8m. Nine players were bought for a total of £6.65m, while fourteen were sold, raising £12.85m. Among the purchases were Nigel Quashie, £2.5m from Queens Park Rangers, and Carlton Palmer, who cost £1.1m from Southampton. Those going the other way included Steve Stone, sold to Aston Villa for £5.5m, Colin Cooper, who cost Middlesbrough £2.5m and Kevin Campbell, who went to the Turkish Club Trabzonspor for £3m.

Forest's 1998–99 Premier League season may have been marked by a rare case of financial discipline off the pitch, but on it the club struggled and was relegated with just 35 points. However, the previous year's operating loss of £4.35m was transformed to a small profit of £407,000 and borrowings were reduced to £1.05m. On the surface, despite relegation, Forest appeared to be in a decent financial state and the directors' decision to hold wages at First Division levels seemed to be vindicated. Behind the scenes, however, a new battle for control of the club was being fought.

It became clear that yet more investment would be needed if Forest were to return to the Premiership and be able to stay there for more than just one season. The club was haemorrhaging cash, with a wage bill that, although reduced, was still in excess of total turnover. An operating loss of £5.66m for the 1999–2000 season and losses incurred in the transfer market left the club with debts of £10.12m by May 2000. Forest finished in fourteenth place in the First Division, way off even a play-off slot. Nigel Doughty now offered to invest £6m in the club, but was not prepared to invest in the plc holding company, which he thought was mismanaged. A vote of shareholders accepted the terms but Scholar and Julian Markham went to court to try and get the vote overturned. The original demand that Doughty's investment be returned was dropped during proceedings and instead the two called for Doughty to be forced to buy their shares.

The case opened on 16 January 2001 and the proceedings revealed an almost unbelievable tale of incompetence and greed. It soon became clear that the reason why Scholar and Markham were opposed to Doughty's investment was that they did not stand to benefit personally from the cash injection. Indeed, that was the very reason why Doughty was insistent that the money went into the club rather than the plc. It also became apparent that one of the main reasons for the board's inertia in attempting to take the club forward was a major falling out between Scholar and Markham, with Phil Soar supporting Scholar. Markham had even taken to recording board meetings secretly as he was convinced that 'there was a group of directors meeting to oust me from the board . . . there was plotting and a conspiracy'.[3]

The court ruled against Scholar and Markham and at the time of writing, Doughty was cleared to take over. Forest sold Jermaine Jenas to Newcastle for £5m in February 2002 and Doughty planned a rights issue to raise an equal amount, which would mainly fall on him as he ended up owning 85 per cent of the club's shares. It is too early to tell whether or not Forest's position will stabilise. Some of the circumstances of the club's decline are almost, but not completely, unique. The battle for control of the club obviously distracted management from addressing the issues that arose from relegation, while the strategy of paying Premier League wages while in the First Division was unsustainable without the financial reserves of a club like Blackburn. The signs are that under the ownership of Doughty and management of Paul Hart, Forest are investing in youth and although the club still hopes to return to the Premiership, it will not put its very existence in danger trying to do so.

Manchester City are the only club currently in the Premiership that have been relegated from it and fallen as low as the Second Division yet managed to return. In the ten-year history of the Premier League, Manchester City have spent five seasons in it, four in the First Division and one in the Second. City's slide from the Premier League to the Second Division started at the end of the 1996 season when Alan Ball's team finished eighteenth. The following season saw the sacking of Ball, followed shortly by the resignation of his successor Steve Coppell and the six-week reign of Phil Neal before Frank Clark was appointed just after Christmas 1996. Clark brought in five players, including Kevin Horlock from Swindon for £1.25m, and sold four, among them Steve Lomas to West Ham for £1.6m. Before Clark arrived Niall Quinn had been sold to Sunderland for £1.3m and at the end of the season City had a small transfer deficit of £800,000. Attendances held up quite well considering relegation, and turnover actually increased slightly to £12.72m. The most dramatic effect of relegation was an increase in the wage bill from £6.43m to £7.2m. Given the upheaval of the 1996–97 season, with four different managers, it was no surprise that the club failed to win promotion and finished mid-table. The following season Clark invested heavily in strengthening his squad for a push for promotion. In came 11 new players, including the £3m Lee Bradbury from Portsmouth, and 8 were sold. In an attempt to keep costs under control, 21 players were loaned out over the season and at the end of it 15 were released but the wage bill still increased to £11.8m. Despite the investment in players City were relegated on the last day of the season, winning 5–2 away at Stoke.

For Manchester City, joining the Second Division in 1998 was the lowest point in the club's 104-year history. Joe Royle had been appointed as manager in February but was unable to avoid relegation. Georgi Kinkladze was sold to Ajax for £5m once relegation had been assured and Royle embarked on a massive clearout, releasing the fifteen players with another eight players sold before Christmas 1998. Although the 1997–98 season was a disaster on the pitch, amazingly revenue increased to £15.2m, mainly as a result of a 6 per cent increase in attendances. Royle's clearout had the desired effect on the wage bill, which was slashed from £11.5m to £6.89m, while surprisingly turnover only fell to £12.73m, still more than when the club was last in the Premier League. City achieved promotion by the skin of their teeth thanks to an amazing play-off final against Gillingham. The match was goalless until the 81st minute when Asaba put Gillingham in front and many thought the Gills had sewn up the match when Taylor added a second with only four minutes of normal time remaining. However, in the 89th minute Horlock got one back and then, deep into injury time, Dickov scored an equaliser. Extra time was scoreless and City completed one of the great comebacks by winning the penalty shoot-out.

Manchester City's return to the First Division saw the club adopt a cautious approach with only three players signed and nine sold or released. The wage bill increased once more by £2.6m, but that was more than offset by an increase in turnover of £4.78m. The increase in turnover came from an improved share of the Football League television contract and a 13.5 per cent increase in attendances. City achieved automatic promotion back to the Premiership in 2000, behind Charlton, and were determined to stay up. Alfe Inge Harland from Leeds and Spencer Prior from Derby were bought at the end of the 1999–2000 season but once the new season was under way Royle soon realised that he would have to spend to have a chance of staying up. At £3.65m Paulo Wanchope from West Ham was the most expensive of eight signings that cost a total of £13.25m. The highest-profile arrival at Maine Road, however, cost nothing. Former AC Milan star and World Player of the Year George Weah may have been a free transfer but his wages were reported to be in the region of £40,000 a week, taking the wage bill to £9.48m – still less than the wage bill City took down to the Second Division.

Despite a substantial investment in the squad, Manchester City's 2000–01 season was a failure and they returned to the First Division after finishing 18th with just 34 points. The season was, however, the most lucrative in the club's history and turnover was £32.36m, compared to £12.67m when they last played in the Premier League six seasons previously. The enhanced income meant that the club was not only able to comfortably afford an £18.1m wage bill, but was able to report a £5.4m operating profit. This would help City keep most of the squad intact for the coming First Division season.

After relegation, Joe Royle was replaced by Kevin Keegan who set about building a team in his own image. Keegan bought 11 players throughout the season for a total of £12.2m, with John Maken the most expensive at £5m from Preston. The effect on the wage bill is unknown at the time of writing, but it is expected to be higher than it was during the previous Premier League season. Chairman David Bernstein explained: 'The short-term effects of this policy will result in sizeable losses but I believe that our shareholders and supporters would want us to focus on the longer-term opportunities and upsides.'[4] The upsides being promotion back to the Premiership, which was achieved as First Division Champions.

City's slide from the Premier League to the Second Division occurred against a backdrop of boardroom infighting and a succession of managers. The infighting was the result of the 1994 takeover of the club by former Maine Road hero Francis Lee who ousted long-time Chairman Peter Swales but was left with Swales's staunch ally Stephen Boler as a majority shareholder. He died in 1998. Lee's popularity with the fans nose-dived after the club was relegated from the Premier League and eventually he was replaced by the former chairman of fashion retailer French Connection, avid City supporter David Bernstein. Bernstein delivered some much-needed stability to the boardroom of the club and under Royle the club was able to plot its return to the top flight. Royle served City for 36 months, the longest tenure of a Manchester City manager after Tony Brook, who resigned in 1979 – since then 14 managers had occupied what had become a very hot seat.

It was neither Bernstein nor Royle who were responsible for Manchester City's bounce back from Second Division oblivion to the Premier League, however, it was the club's fans. When City were in the Second Division for the 1998–99 season their average home attendance was 28,273, more than double the next best supported club in the division, Stoke City, and more than any other First Division club bar Sunderland. With Sunderland promoted when City rejoined the First Division, their average home gate, at 32,088, was over 10,000 more than nearest rival Birmingham City. The financial advantage that level of support gave the club over its rivals is even more dramatic. In their Second Division season City earned a total of £12.72m when its nearest competitor, Preston North End, turned over £5.13m and the average for the division was just £3.6m. The following season in the First Division Manchester City's income was again streets ahead of the opposition's at £17.5m, compared to next best Bolton's £13.43m and a divisional average of just £7.73m. Given the relative paucity of the Football League television revenue, compared to the Premier League, the example of Manchester City shows that a strong supporter base is the key to recovery for clubs relegated from the Premier League and even from the First Division. That the board was able to harness that support and translate financial dominance into results on the pitch deserves credit, but the fact that it took a penalty shoot-out against a club that earned just over a quarter of what City did illustrates how tenuous is the link between financial strength and playing success.

Queens Park Rangers and Swindon Town are the only other two clubs that have been relegated from the Premier League and sunk to the depths of the Second Division. Unlike Manchester City, however, neither QPR nor Swindon were able to bounce back to the Premiership and both have been plunged into administration. QPR were a founder member of the Premier League and finished fifth in its first season under the management of Gerry Francis. Francis left to manage Tottenham in November 1994 to be replaced by Ray Wilkins, and in 1996 Rangers were relegated after finishing bottom of the then 22-club Premiership with just 30 points. Wilkins was replaced by Stuart Houston who strengthened his squad with John Spencer and Gavin Peacock from Chelsea, and Mike Sheron from

Stoke City for a total of £5.65m. Matthew Rose and keeper Lee Harper were bought from Arsenal for £625,000 as QPR's wage bill increased by £2m. Houston's side finished mid-table and by November 1997 he was shown the door. Ray Harford took over QPR in December 1997 and trimmed the squad, raising £5m by selling Andy Impey and Trevor Sinclair to West Ham and John Spencer to Everton. Players were brought in on low fees and free transfers, including Vinnie Jones from Wimbledon for £750,000, but the wage bill escalated to £9.82m, which was £2.25m more than turnover. If the QPR board thought that it was worth making a loss for a season to secure a return to the Premiership they were wrong – Harford's team only just managed to avoid relegation, finishing 21st. Having failed to deliver promotion Harford made way for the return of Gerry Francis. With a wage bill in excess of income Francis sought to make ends meet by selling Sheron to Barnsley and Nigel Quashie to Nottingham Forest for a total of £4m, while spending just £700,000 on three players, and signing West Ham keeper Ludek Miklosko on a free transfer. The money raised was essential as the wage bill had been trimmed by half a million to £8.76m, but turnover fell even further to £5.12m because QPR no longer qualified for the Premier League parachute payment and they had suffered a 10 per cent fall in attendances. On the pitch it could be said that their performance improved as they finished one place higher than the previous season in 20th place. The following season brought some hope for the long-suffering Rangers fans. Few players were traded as Francis steadied the ship and the following season could be faced with confidence as the team briefly challenged for a play-off place before finishing tenth. Far from being the season of QPR's triumphant return to the top flight, the 2000 01 season was a disaster, on and off the pitch. Relegation to the Second Division looked a certainty well before the season's end and Ian Holloway replaced Francis in January 2001. In the four seasons since relegation from the Premiership QPR had run up combined operating losses of nearly £20m and with the Second Division looming they entered administration in April 2001.

There are plenty of other issues that may have contributed to QPR's decline: the flotation on the stock market as Loftus Road plc in October 1996 that raised £12m and the fluctuating fortunes of owner Chris Wright's business Chrysalis, spring to mind. There has also been talk over the years about the club selling their west London ground for redevelopment and moving to a purpose-built stadium near Heathrow or even Milton Keynes. There have also been talks about a merger with Wimbledon and a ground share with Brentford. But the fundamental causes of QPR's financial decline were too many players being paid too much money for too long, and not enough people paying to watch them. Prior to the formation of the Premier League in 1992, QPR's average gate was steady at around 13,500. The first season of the Premiership saw an increase to 15,000 and reached 15,672 for the club's last Premiership season of 1995–96. Relegation saw gates fall back to 12,554 and since then attendances have fluctuated between a high of 13,083 in 1997–98 to a low of 11,749 last season. What is clear is that QPR's natural level of support is between 12,000 and 13,000, which, while playing in the Football League, will generate income of between five and six million pounds a year. While in administration, the club has been forced to operate within these constraints and has now emerged as a leaner, if not fitter, operation. QPR's post-relegation wage bills of around £9m were clearly unsustainable. However, that is not to attach any blame to the club's board or management as the bulk of the players – with the exception of Ray Wilkins' Chelsea signings, who were such a drain on the limited resources – were signed during the Premier League campaign. The length of their contracts, between three and five years, meant that they could not be released but had to be found other clubs. The inflexibility of player contracts is another major contributory factor in the relegation-to-administration journey of QPR, and one that affects all clubs who find themselves in the reduced circumstances of the Football League.

Unlike Manchester City or QPR, Swindon Town had no experience of top-flight football when they were promoted to the Premier League via the play-offs in 1993. In fact, before reaching the old Second Division in 1987, the club had only spent seven seasons outside of the bottom two divisions since joining the Third Division South in 1920. Swindon's rise from the Fourth Division to the Premier League in nine seasons was therefore a considerable achievement. The rise under the management of firstly Lou Macari, then Ossie Ardiles and finally Glenn Hoddle, also enhanced the reputations of those three managers, who all went on to greater things. Indeed Glenn Hoddle didn't even wait to see Swindon compete in the Premier League after taking them there, moving to Chelsea in the close season. Hoddle's successor John Gorman didn't spend heavily in the transfer market and once the club was relegated Nicky Summerbee was offloaded to Manchester City for £1.5m, giving Swindon a player-trading surplus of £1.5m for the season.

Swindon's administration of February 2000 was not the result of a club trying to maintain a Premier League wage bill carried into the First Division, but rather a case of it amassing debt as a result of paying a high wage bill once relegated in an attempt to buy a Premier League place. As then Swindon Chairman Cliff Puffett put it in an article in the *Sporting Life* on 3 February 2000: 'We tried to chase the dream of returning to the Premiership, but it didn't work. That involved a massive financial commitment, especially in terms of players' wages.' That commitment cost £16m over the five years between relegation and 1999, the last time the club filed any accounts. Over that time total turnover was £23.5m and accumulated losses reached £2.37m. Like QPR and unlike Manchester City, Swindon did not have the supporter base to be able to sustain losses over time. When Swindon were promoted to the Premier League, attendances shot up from an average 10,567 to 15,011. Upon relegation they fell back down to 9,408. The people of Swindon would obviously rather watch a winning team in the Second Division than a losing one in the First as attendances rose to 10,040 in the 1995–96 season when Swindon won promotion back to the First Division as champions. Since then, though, Swindon have not been a winning team and attendances have continually fallen, to the point that only an average 6,354 watched Town finish 13th in the Second Division last season.

It may appear from the above that relegation from the Premier League is a death knell for most clubs but a number of clubs have dealt with the situation and bounced back stronger, the most notable of examples being Sunderland and Charlton Athletic. In fact they are really the only true examples as Middlesbrough and Blackburn have relied on benefactor funding and have therefore been able to buy promotion after relegation with little regard to the cost. Sunderland and Charlton, however, are both listed on the stock exchange and although they both have wealthy shareholders, they also rely on support from institutional investors and small shareholders and are run as businesses with at least the appearance of hopefully making profits.

Sunderland are the third best-supported club in England. With an average home attendance of 46,744 for the 2001–02 season, only

Newcastle with 51,373 and Manchester United with 67,558, drew more fans through the turnstiles in the Premier League's tenth season. Naturally, supporters of other clubs will dispute Sunderland's status, as will other club's chairmen. Sunderland don't have a record of success anything like as impressive as that of Arsenal or Liverpool, or even Tottenham Hotspur, Newcastle United, Chelsea or Leeds United. Sunderland may have won six League titles, but the last was in 1936, although they can claim two further League championships for 1999 and 1996 after the formation of the Premier League. Winning the FA Cup for the second time in 1973, having previously lifted the trophy in 1937, represents their most recent triumph and their 2–0 defeat by Liverpool in the 1992 FA Cup final was the last time they contested a major final. Other clubs will argue that they have many more passive supporters, who watch most of their matches on television, buy merchandise and subscribe to the club website. But by the simple measure of how many people actually pay to spend every other Saturday for nine months of the year watching their team, Sunderland are the third best-supported club in England. It was not always thus and that support has yet to be translated into economic or competitive advantage. The eight clubs listed above all turned over more money than Sunderland in the 2000–01 season and all finished higher in the Premier League final table.

Sunderland offer a good example of a club dealing with relegation from the Premier League without plunging into an almost terminal crisis. When they were relegated after just one season in the Premier League in 1997 it seemed as if all the effort that had got them back into the top flight after a six-year absence had been wasted. In the 20 seasons that preceded the 1992 formation of the Premier League, Sunderland spent only seven of them in the First Division, twelve in the Second and the other one in Division Three. That Sunderland managed their relegation from the Premier League as well as they did should come as no surprise – the 20-year period prior to the Premier League's formation saw them deal with relegation four times. But, as has been shown, the consequences of relegation from the top flight in the Premiership era are more serious than they have been previously and it has been a blow from which many clubs have been unable to recover.

Sunderland were relegated from the Premier League on the last day of the season in 1997 and the timing was more than a little inconvenient. The club was preparing to move into a new stadium, the Stadium of Light, after 99 years at Roker Park. The Stadium of Light was the realised dream of Chairman Bob Murray and Chief Executive John Fickling who had taken Sunderland to the stock market the previous December and raised the necessary £10m to build the stadium. It was to become the building block for Sunderland's subsequent success, but in 1997 the club had the problem of having to deal with an unexpected relegation. In a television documentary that recorded the club's 1996–97 Premier League season, Murray was seen to ban the 'R' word from the vocabulary of Sunderland's staff as relegation went from being a probability to a distinct possibility and it appeared that relegation was the one eventuality for which the busy board had not planned. But it was away at Wimbledon that Sunderland went down to an 85th minute goal by Jason Euell and Sunderland moved into the best stadium in the First Division.

Despite relegation, Sunderland's gates improved by a massive 65 per cent when they played their first season in the Stadium of Light. The increase in attendances afforded by the new stadium was immediately translated into the bottom line. Sunderland must be the only club to be relegated from the Premier League and then see turnover increase by 40 per cent. In 1998 Sunderland earned £18.25m in the First Division at the Stadium of Light, while in the previous year they earned £13.15m in the Premier League at Roker Park, with an average attendance of 34,337 as opposed to 20,847. The increase in income allowed Peter Reid to strengthen the squad and 11 players were bought and 11 sold for a net cost of £2.57m. There was a concomitant increase in the wage bill too, up by £2.46m to £8.16m. Significantly, Sunderland's wage bill was not the Division's highest. Middlesbrough (£11.41m), QPR (£9.82m), Nottingham Forest (£9.71m), Manchester City (£8.74m) and Sheffield United (£8.3m) all had higher wage bills than Sunderland but none of them had as much income.

Despite the massive support and a strengthened squad, Sunderland narrowly missed out on a return to the Premiership after a dramatic play-off final which Charlton won on penalties. The disappointment of the failure to regain a Premier League place did not, however, dampen the enthusiasm of Sunderland's fans and the following season saw another increase in attendances, up by 12 per cent to 38,745. Reid resisted the temptation to rebuild the team completely, adding just three players at a cost of £2.2m. The wage bill went up to £10m but the increased crowds more than compensated, driving up income to £24.08m. Sunderland romped into the First Division in 1999, winning the championship, and more importantly promotion back to the Premier League, with 105 points.

If Sunderland's financial policy in the face of relegation from the Premier League can be described as cautious, the club's reaction to promotion was anything but. As the squad that won promotion was similar to the one that had been relegated two years previously, it was clear that in order to consolidate Premiership status some new blood would have to be bought in. Reid spent £10m on ten new players, with £4m going to Valencia for Stefan Schwarz and £2.2m to West Bromwich Albion for Kevin Kilbane. The purchases were countered by the sale of 11 players for a total of £8.2m with Michael Bridges going to Leeds for £5m and Kevin Ball and Lee Clark joining Fulham for a combined £3.2m. There was a massive increase in Sunderland's wage bill, up 121 per cent to £22.14m, but with the enhanced TV money from the Premier League and increased capacity at the Stadium of Light, income rose by 55 per cent to £37.3m. With the Premier League's eleventh highest wage bill and eighth highest income, English football's third best-supported club finished seventh.

It is too early to see whether Sunderland have consolidated their position in the top flight. The club finished seventh again in 2001 but only avoided relegation in 2002 by four points, but the point is that Sunderland survived relegation from the Premier League in 1997 and came back stronger. Sound financial management and a refusal to panic and overspend on wages and transfers are part of the reason why relegation was not the crisis for Sunderland that it was for other clubs, but the main reason was the level of support the club enjoyed in the First Division. Sunderland therefore reaped the benefit of investing in the bricks and mortar of the Stadium of Light as opposed to players. The cornerstone of Sunderland's success only cost £9m to build, which would only buy one or two players. It was not a case of building a stadium and just waiting for the fans to turn up, however. Sunderland worked very hard to build a supporter base, offering substantial discounts to children and keeping season-ticket prices at reasonable levels, something they were only able to do as a result of the capacity afforded by the stadium. Sunderland's success could not be replicated by a club without the same level of support or a stadium large enough to accommodate it, but that is not to say that a club without those is necessarily doomed when relegated from the Premiership, as the example of Charlton shows.

When the FA's independent tribunal ruled that Wimbledon could move to Milton Keynes it claimed that the club's situation was unique in that it did not have its own stadium and was losing money. The tribunal must have forgotten about Charlton who played away from the Valley for seven years from 1985. The reasons why the Charlton board abandoned the Valley have never really been made clear; there were safety issues and the club could not afford to renovate the crumbling terracing, but there were also issues of ownership. What is salutary about the Charlton story is not why the club left the Valley in the first place, but how Charlton's supporters achieved the return of 1992. The campaign had a political dimension as the supporters formed a political party, the Valley Party, which fielded 60 candidates in the 1990 local elections, winning 10 per cent of the vote. The fans also raised £1m to fund renovation of the ground and when work was needed to get it ready for the return, rolled up their sleeves and did it themselves.

When Charlton achieved promotion to the Premier League in 1990, top-flight football returned to the Valley for the first time in 41 years. Attendances shot up by nearly 50 per cent to 19,825, 99 per cent of capacity. At £8.22m, Charlton had the lowest wage bill in the Premiership and at £16.27m the third-lowest income. There was not much that Charlton could do to increase earnings as they could not fit any more supporters into the Valley and the ground had proved more than adequate for the club's First Division level of support, which was around 13,000. One option would have been to dramatically increase ticket prices but the board saw promotion to the Premier League as an opportunity to build a larger loyal supporter base and kept season-ticket prices reasonable. When the club was relegated after a season in the Premier League 15,000 season tickets were sold for the First Division campaign, compared to the 5,500 sold two years previously. As a result attendances only slipped marginally to 19,558, which could be attributed to lower sales to visiting fans. So on their return to the First Division Charlton were the Division's fourth best-supported club. The increased support was translated into revenue and with turnover of £11.75m Charlton were also the fourth wealthiest First Division club. This enabled the club to sustain its Premier League wage bill without plunging into the red, and only Blackburn Rovers paid more in wages in the 1999–2000 First Division season. With continuity and a few canny buys Alan Curbishley was able to plot an immediate return, which was achieved as champions in 2000. Like Reid at Sunderland, Curbishley knew that he would have to invest to strengthen his squad in order to consolidate Premier League status, and in 2000, £11m was spent on nine players, with Claus Jensen at £4m from Bolton and Jonatan Johansson at £3.75m from Rangers the most expensive. Tellingly Charlton's wage bill increased by 55 per cent to £17.07m, but it was still the third lowest in the Premiership, and finishing positions of ninth and fourteenth since promotion suggest that the club is punching slightly above its weight. Of course, Charlton could be relegated again, but they have shown that they are capable of surviving it.

Relegation from the Premier League has had disastrous consequences for clubs like Nottingham Forest, Swindon, Bradford City and Queens Park Rangers, but the experiences of Manchester City, Sunderland and Charlton show that it does not always have to be the case. Manchester City and Sunderland have survived because of their high level of support: traditional in City's case, built by the club in Sunderland's. Charlton have also succeeded because of their support, which they have treated with a respect that has been reciprocated. The clear lesson is that away from the Premier League's television riches, bums on seats become the clubs' strength and the key to their survival. Once again it is proved that the most important element of a football club is its fans.

## ENDNOTES

[1] Discerning Eye (www.theeye.com). Chancery Tales: The Litigation Saga.
[2] Ibid.
[3] Ibid.
[4] Manchester City plc. 18 January 2002. Interim results announcement, Chairman's statement.

# 5. Debt

THE MASSIVE INCREASE IN MONEY EARNED BY ENGLISH FOOTBALL IN THE 1990s WAS accompanied by a massive increase in debt. By 2001 the combined income of the 20 Premier League clubs had reached £907.4m, while combined net debt had risen to £377.8m. In the Football League, turnover was £268.89m and borrowings were £307.88m. Every one of the 92 clubs in the Premier and Football Leagues is different, not just in terms of their history and heritage, but also in terms of their development as businesses. It is therefore impossible to generalise about the financial state of English football beyond a few simple observations:

- In 2001 Premier League clubs' combined annual income was 2.4 times their collective debt, while in the Football League debt was 14.5 per cent more than annual income.
- The First Division accounted for £223.05m (70 per cent) of the Football League's collective debt, but only 66 per cent of its income.
- First Division debt was 1.24 times annual income.

Some of the clubs with high debt levels in the First Division were underwritten by wealthy individuals, such as Fulham's Mohamed Al-Fayed, who had bankrolled the club to the tune of £65.5m as part of a (successful) strategy to buy a way into the Premier League, and Wolves, where Sir Jack Hayward had underwritten loans totalling £33m in a failed attempt to do the same. Other clubs, such as Nottingham Forest and Queens Park Rangers, had accumulated debts after they were relegated from the Premier League and continued to pay top-flight wages while earning greatly reduced First Division incomes. Before looking at some of the issues raised by English football's indebtedness, it is worth looking in some detail at those clubs with the greatest debt levels as they show not just how debt can be incurred, but also the strategic thinking that leads to its accumulation.

By the summer of 2001, the two clubs with the biggest debt levels in English football were Chelsea and Leeds United. Chelsea had around £102m of long- and short-term debt, while Leeds United had around £70m of borrowings. Leeds United and Chelsea are very similar clubs, both in terms of current profile and status and also their previous histories. Both have finished in the top six in each of the last five seasons and enjoyed extended European campaigns. Most would now consider both to be part of English football's elite, but both have had periods outside of the top flight in the past. Leeds have spent 51 seasons in the top flight and 27 seasons outside it, while Chelsea, with the benefit of being founded 14 years before the Yorkshire club, have spent 67 seasons in the top division and 19 outside it. Leeds have the edge when it comes to League titles with three – 1969, 1974 and 1992 – compared to Chelsea's solitary 1955 title. However, Chelsea have won three FA Cups (1970, 1997 and 2000) to Leeds' one (1972). In Europe, Leeds have won the Fairs Cup, which later became the UEFA Cup, twice (1968 and 1971), while Chelsea lifted the Cup-Winners' Cup in 1998. On the downside, Leeds spent between 1983 and 1990 in the Second Division and Chelsea became a classic yo-yo club in the 1970s and '80s spending 8 out of 14 seasons in the Second Division between 1975 and 1989. Both clubs have enjoyed roughly the same levels of attendance, although analysis is complicated by the limits on capacity, league played in and national trends in overall football attendance. As English football club brands, Leeds United and Chelsea would seem to be closely matched.

Leeds and Chelsea also have much in common as businesses. Both clubs are quoted on the stock market with Leeds joining the main market in August 1996, as Leeds Sporting plc, and Chelsea gaining admission to the junior Alternative Investment Market as Chelsea Village plc five months earlier. Both clubs also have 'strategic alliances' with Rupert Murdoch's BSkyB to exploit certain commercial rights. But there the similarities end.

Leeds United and Chelsea both have the same strategic objective, to become established top-flight European clubs, but have sought to achieve it through adopting totally different strategies. Broadly speaking, it is fair to say that Leeds' strategy is football focused while Chelsea's is more broad based, encompassing hotel, leisure, travel and other businesses. These differences are graphically illustrated by a comparative analysis of both clubs' annual results for the year 2001.

In terms of on-pitch performance, Leeds had a far more successful 2000–01 season than Chelsea, finishing fourth in the Premier League, two places above Chelsea, and progressing to the semi-final stage of the Champions League, while Chelsea were knocked out of the first round of the UEFA Cup by lowly St Galen. In the domestic Cups, Leeds were knocked out of both League and FA Cups in the fourth round, while Chelsea managed to reach the fifth round of the FA Cup, but were also eliminated from the League Cup in the fourth round. But Chelsea earned more money: £93.63m from all operations compared to Leeds' £86.25m income. Further inspection reveals that Chelsea owed their superior income to the performance of their non-football subsidiaries, of which they have twelve, that had a combined turnover of £43.39m, 46.4 per cent of total earnings. Leeds have just one non-football subsidiary, a travel company that contributed £10.7m, 12.5 per cent of income. If non-football operations and merchandising sales are stripped out, Leeds had income totalling £69.18m, compared to Chelsea's £45.52m. Around £18m of this difference can be ascribed to Leeds' Champions League run, illustrating the financial importance of that competition and explaining why Leeds were able to report pre-player trading, pre-tax operating profits of over £10m, while Chelsea reported a pre-player trading, pre-tax operating loss of £6.8m. Before assessing the relative merits of each club's strategy it is worth looking at how they evolved.

Having won the last First Division title in 1992, Leeds were an established Premier League club when long-standing Chairman Leslie Silver retired in 1996. Silver's retirement sparked off an acrimonious takeover battle for the club, with the London-based Caspian and Conrad group, headed by stock market darling Chris Ackers, lined up against Barry Rubery, majority shareholder of satellite decoder manufacturer Pace Micro Technology. The Leeds board were split with Silver and Managing Director Bill Fotherby in favour of the Caspian bid and Peter Gilman supporting Rubery. On 3 July it was announced that the club had been sold to Caspian for £35m and Gilman responded by saying the deal 'stinks for the fans and undervalues the club'.[1] Considering that when Leeds joined the stock market the following month they were capitalised at £52.7m, he may have had a point. Rubery went on to buy Huddersfield Town for a reported £8m in 1999, a deal that turned sour and saw him exit the club in January 2002, after overseeing the club's relegation to the Second Division with increased debts. Rubery, whose company also manufactured the ITV Digital set-top boxes, also found time to be one of the five signatories to the ill-fated ITV Digital/Football League TV deal. Perhaps Leeds had a lucky escape. Gilman sought recourse to the High Court, claiming that any deal had to be unanimously accepted by the board, but Mr Justice Rattee found in Caspian's favour.

Caspian's strategy was to create 'one of Europe's leading vertically integrated sports, media and leisure groups, capable of delivering shareholder value in the medium to long term'. The company's annual report of the following year explained how the acquisition of Leeds fitted into this 'bold new strategy'.

> Fundamental to the Board's strategy is the broadening of the business base of LUH (Leeds United Holdings plc) into other sports and ancillary commercial leisure activities. At the time of the acquisition of the football club, the Board is determined to use its best endeavours to exploit the latent development potential of the 50-acre Elland Road site.[2]

This would be done through the building of a 14,000-seat 'Arena', adjacent to the stadium's West Stand, 'capable of being transformed from either an NHL-style ice hockey arena or an NBA-type basketball court with a capacity of 14,000 into a pop, rock or classical concert venue'. Caspian also had plans to use the Arena for conferences and exhibitions and build a 200-bed hotel, as well as changing the name of the company to Leeds Sporting.

The Arena project caught the spirit of the age. Many other clubs, including Chelsea, Aston Villa and Sheffield United, thought that they could utilise the land around their stadia to build other businesses that would ultimately fund the football club. However, in the summer of 1997 many Leeds fans were dismayed that the club had had yet another disappointing season, finishing 11th in the Premiership, and thought that money spent on the Arena project would have been better spent by George Graham on strengthening the squad. Ackers sought to reassure them that:

> . . . when the Arena is operational, the revenue and profits it generates will flow back into the football, so by the turn of the century, I would like to contend that the Arena will be contributing to the continued success and further success of the football club.[3]

He added that the project was separately funded.

Ackers stood down in July to be replaced by Peter Ridsdale, a life-long fan with a successful retail career behind him. Ackers went on to found the Sports Internet Group and Ridsdale at first pledged to continue with the Arena project. However, by October 2000, Ridsdale reported that 'in the context of a significant softening of the market for commercial leisure development in the Leeds area, we have concluded that the scheme as originally contemplated would be unlikely to enhance shareholder value'. Ridsdale added that the club was in discussions with Leeds council about using the land for retail development. By 2002, the plan had been wholly abandoned with the club looking to relocate to a new stadium on the outskirts of the city. The company also changed its name from Leeds Sporting to Leeds United, a move, Ridsdale said, 'which clearly reflects our decision to maximise shareholder value by focusing on football'.[4]

Ridsdale's appointment marked a sea change in the club's strategy. Although subtle at first, increased transfer spending at the same time as a cooling on the Arena project saw the club refocus on its core business: football. Players such as Michael Duberry (£4.5m from Chelsea), Jason Wilcox (£3m from Blackburn Rovers), David Batty (£4.4m from Newcastle), Michael Bridges (£4m from Sunderland) and Darren Huckerby (£4m from Coventry City) were among 13 players added to the Leeds squad between 1998 and 1999, at a total cost of around £20m. With the exception of the £12m sale of Jimmy Floyd Hasselbaink, reluctantly sold after he was unable to agree an improved contract, 20 players were sold for either minimal amounts or given free transfers, raising a total of just £3m.

When interviewed by the author in May 2002 Ridsdale explained the change in strategy: 'I inherited a strategy. Before you can even consider a broad-based strategy you have to be successful at your primary business, which is football.' Some may say that the main difference between Ackers and Ridsdale was the latter was a fan, and a Leeds fan at that, while the former was an entrepreneur who saw football's popularity as a means to an end. But Ridsdale saw a sense of urgency in keeping Leeds near the top of the Premiership so they could regularly compete in Europe. Announcing half-yearly losses of £13.8m in March 2002 Ridsdale explained:

> The long-term future of football revenues will see the dominant clubs within Europe benefiting to the potential detriment of the rest. TV revenues and European-wide competitions will allow the top five or six clubs within the UK to continue to grow their brands and revenues. Our five-year strategy has been to ensure that Leeds United are in a position to capitalise on these changes if and when they occur.

Ridsdale pointed out that in the season before he became chairman Leeds had the lowest ever 'goals for' tally (28) for a club that had avoided relegation from the Premiership:

> Our view was that what we had to have was a business that was in Europe more often than not and that when ultimately TV rights were being negotiated, overseas rights etc, the value was going to be in the brands that were known on a worldwide basis, or at least a pan-European basis.[5]

There is an element of a sink-or-swim mentality in Ridsdale's reasoning – he justifies increased expenditure on players, either through transfer fees or wages or both, not just on the basis of wanting to achieve a certain level of success, but also to avoid the consequences of failure. When he says he sees the 'dominant clubs within Europe benefiting to the potential detriment of the rest' from the increased value of TV rights, it is the 'detriment of the rest' part that is the key. Ridsdale clearly sees that Leeds cannot afford to be lumped in with the rest. This is part of the reason why player-cost inflation is a feature at every level of the game. While clubs towards the bottom of the Premier League attempt to spend their way to safety and avoid relegation, clubs towards the top of the table attempt to spend their way to success and avoid failure. This inflationary dynamic is present in all leagues and is more emphatic the larger the gap between success and failure is. Although salary caps may provide part of the solution, the problem can be only be addressed through closing the gap, i.e. a more equitable distribution of income.

When Ridsdale paid £18m, then a world record for a defender, for Rio Ferdinand from West Ham, many questioned his wisdom. It wasn't just the size of the fee that caused eyebrows to be raised, it was also the deal's timing, at the height of the speculation over the future of the transfer system, as Ridsdale told the author in a personal interview:

> The fact is I had ultimate belief that Rio would be part and parcel of us qualifying for Europe more often and that is where the revenues come from so he pays for himself if we qualify for Europe more often, irrespective of the state of the transfer market. We also wrote into his contract that he couldn't speak to another club for less than a specified sum, which would guarantee a very healthy profit. I also believed that the football business would collapse worldwide if the transfer system was scrapped and I did not believe that the powers that be would let that happen.

It would appear that the 'specified sum' was in the region of £30m – the figure that Manchester United were reported to have paid Leeds for Ferdinand in July 2002. Ridsdale has been vindicated in that Leeds have now qualified for Europe for the last five consecutive seasons, but at a cost.

Since 1997 Leeds' turnover has increased from £23.2m to £86.3m in 2001 but there has not been a corresponding increase in profits, in fact there have been hardly any profits at all. Minimal pre-tax profits in 1998, 1999 and 2000 totalled £2.28m on a combined turnover of £122.5m, but 2001 saw the full impact of the Ferdinand transfer and an increase in wages to £43m, resulting in a pre-tax loss of £7.59m. At the same time Leeds' debts increased to nearly £40m. In common with other clubs with high levels of debt, Leeds have reorganised their borrowings and taken out a long-term loan, secured against future ticket sales. Leeds borrowed £60m at a fixed 7.65 per cent to be paid over 25 years, which means the club will have to find around £4.6m a year in interest payments. Given that Leeds took £15.47m in gate money in the 2000–01 season, that figure should be affordable. However, had that charge applied this year, Leeds' operating profits would have been more than halved. The first fruits of Leeds' financial engineering arrived at Elland Road on 18 October 2001 in the shape of Seth Johnson from Derby, who cost £7m, rising to £9m depending on appearances. Johnson was followed by Robbie Fowler from Liverpool on 27 November with a reported £11m price tag. The £60m long-term loan, which had wiped out a £40m short-term debt, had released £20m for transfer spending. Within nine weeks of the details of the loan being announced to the stock exchange, £18m of it had been spent on players.

Debt is debt, whether it is long term or short term, but long-term debt is easier to manage. Ridsdale is unconcerned with club's debt level as he believes that he can always sell players to ease the situation. 'We have a squad that has been independently valued at £220m and frankly we could write the debt off tomorrow if we sold three players.' Ridsdale believes that his squad at the end of the 2001–02 had four players too many, partly due to having to buy cover for injuries and the absence of players involved in the infamous trial and also because the opportunity to buy Robbie Fowler arose, an opportunity that he felt was too good to miss. He has said that he will look to recoup some of the recent spending through sales in the summer, with Olivier Dacourt likely to be one of those sold.

Clearly, Ridsdale has developed a strategy that is primarily football focused and Leeds fans will be glad of that. Shareholders are supportive, although the dismal performance of the club's shares gives them little choice but to hang on as to sell would realise substantial losses. As Ridsdale is only halfway through a five-year plan, the jury must remain out as to whether he has achieved the goals he set himself. But there can be no doubt that Leeds are currently a 'big club'. Ridsdale is realistic about the club's status:

> People talk about big clubs and small clubs, they say there are some big clubs in the First Division and some small clubs in the Premiership. I don't buy that; the only thing that defines whether you are a big club is how you perform today. When we were in the Second Division for eight years we weren't a big club, we were a Second Division club. There are some clubs who aspire to be big clubs, and maybe historically they have been. So I've never been so arrogant as to say we are a big club; we're not. We're just a club that has been reasonably successful for five years without actually winning anything. The next five years could be very good or disastrous – that will depend on management.

Chelsea's strategy, as explained in the Chelsea Village annual report of 2001, is: 'To create a world class stadium at Stamford Bridge, a world class team worthy of consistently playing in the European top flight, and diversify revenue streams away from the core football brand.'[6] Anyone who has recently visited Stamford Bridge will testify that the first objective has been achieved, with a fine stadium finally complete after the opening of the West Stand in time for the start of the 2001–02 season. The team has also undergone a transformation from the yo-yo team of the '70s and '80s to a collection of world-class stars that consistently challenges for European honours and has finished in the top six of the Premiership in each of the last six seasons. The third objective, however, has yet to be achieved and there are reasons to believe that the very existence of that objective could undermine the progress that has been made with the stadium and the team.

Like Leeds, Chelsea's plan was to build diverse revenue streams that would ultimately subsidise the football team. After a protracted legal battle with property developers Cabra Estates, Chairman Ken Bates secured the freehold to Stamford Bridge in 1991 which gave him the means to achieve his objectives. With attendances hovering around the 18,000 mark, the club had shaken off its yo-yo tag and for the following six years finished 11th 4 times and 14th twice – respectable but hardly a springboard to challenge for European honours. The introduction to AIM in March 1996 widened the ownership base but didn't actually raise any money for the company. Bates realised that in order to develop Stamford Bridge he would need a substantial amount of money and his method of raising this was unique: the placing of a £75m Eurobond in December 1997. Arranged by SBC Warburg Dillon Read and Mees Pierson, the bond offered investors an annual rate of return of 8.875 per cent and their capital back after ten years. The bonds could be traded and have proved attractive to investors as interest rates have stayed low. The benefit for Chelsea was that it received the £75m it needed to build two hotels and various other subsidiary businesses and only had to pay back the interest, £6.67m a year. After ten years the club would have to pay back the £75m, but the plan was that by that time the hotels and other businesses would be generating profits and if the capital was not available, they could be remortgaged or even sold. Fundamental to the plan was that the non-football businesses would produce profits that would subsidise the football team. Unfortunately, those businesses have so far failed to deliver.

In the annual report of 2001 Chelsea Village listed seven different revenue streams. Football activities contributed £50.22m of the total £93.63m turnover and made a £4.5m loss. The travel agency contributed £26.24m and made a £685,000 loss. Property sales and leasing fared better, but turnover was only £145,000 and profits were just £42,000. The hotel business earned £11.91m and made a £57,000 loss. Other businesses, including car-parking and events were the most profitable arms of Chelsea's businesses, making a profit of £248,000 on turnover of £417,000. All together, when 'central group costs' of £816,000 and what is called 'leisure services pre-opening costs' were added, the different businesses made a total loss of £6.83m on turnover of £93.73m. Then of course there was the interest on the Eurobond, which when set against interest earned from funds on deposit of £1.97m, ran to £4.6m. In total, Chelsea Village recorded a pre-tax loss of £11.09m, the largest in the club's history.

Bates defended the losses saying that there were some exceptional circumstances: the cost of paying off the sacked coach Gianluca Vialli and his staff amounted to £3m. Chelsea's dismal UEFA Cup campaign, which saw them knocked out in the first round by the lowly Swiss club St Galen, was not down to Bates, nor was the fact that they failed to qualify for the Champions League. 'It's not my fault we didn't qualify for the Champions League. In the 20 years I've been here, I've never even missed a penalty,' he was reported saying by the *London Evening Standard* of 15 October 2001.

The 2001 losses did not occur in isolation. In the previous five years Chelsea Village only made a pre-tax profit in 1998, when victory in the League and Cup-Winners' Cups was supplemented by the sale of apartments to record a profit of £2.1m. Bates fiercely defends his strategy and claims that the losses are often the result of events outside of the company's control. There have been countless delays to the building of the hotels and the opening of the nightclubs and bars because of planning and licensing difficulties. The building work was held up by disputes with contractors, and local environmentalists even managed to find a rare breed of butterfly on the site when objecting to the development. The acquisition of travel company Elizabeth Duff Travel in July 1987 led to legal action by the club claiming that the vendor had misrepresented the true state of the business. In the latest interim results, Bates warns that both the travel and hotel businesses could suffer as a result of the tragedy of 11 September 2001. Taken together these issues graphically illustrate the perils of diversification away from the core business of football.

There is a certain irony in that on the football side Chelsea have been an unmitigated success, yet their ancillary businesses have yet to deliver. The team have recently won numerous trophies – the Cup-Winners' Cup, two FA Cups, the European Supercup and the League Cup – and have been a consistent serious challenger for the Premiership title. Of course these achievements have been made possible only because of a substantial investment in the playing squad both in terms of transfer fees and player wages.

Player wages in 2000 were £37.2m, second only to Manchester United (£44.77m) and Liverpool (£40.12m) and rose to £38.8m in 2001, representing 75 per cent of football turnover. The Eurobond was issued with a condition that none of the proceeds would be spent on players and as none of the subsidiary companies have made a significant contribution to the club's coffers it can surely be argued that the same level of playing performance could have been achieved without the diversification into the hotel and travel business. Moreover, it could be argued that the company should have concentrated on increasing Stamford Bridge's capacity from day one, thereby being able to cash in on the club's new-found popularity and even possibly keeping admission prices within the reach of the club's traditional support.

When the Eurobond matures in 2007, Chelsea will have to find £75m, which should not be too much of a problem. Like Ridsdale, Bates could sell some players, although it could be argued that Chelsea do not have four or five players of sufficient value that they could sell, while still maintaining the same competitive edge. Another option would be to sell the two hotels, which would be contingent on the state of the leisure-property market at the time. Similarly, the travel business could be sold, although it is unlikely that the proceeds would come to £75m. Alternatively, the hotels could be remortgaged, but that would still leave Chelsea having to pay interest payments for the term of the loan. The problem with these options would be that they would seriously undermine the wisdom of the strategy of diversification, which can only be vindicated if the subsidiary businesses start to deliver profits in excess of the annual £7m Eurobond interest payment. Ultimately, however, on-pitch performance will be the key: if

Chelsea become regular Champions League contenders they will earn enough money to pay the interest on the Eurobond and still make profits for shareholders.

We see then, that while Leeds and Chelsea have adopted different strategies, they both have to maintain their positions in the Premiership's elite, and qualify for Europe, preferably the Champions League, for those strategies to be vindicated. This is refreshing news for traditional football supporters. Despite the complexities of the modern football business, success flows directly from on-pitch performance, which, as Ridsdale says, is down to management.

At first glance there would appear to be an air of complacency about both clubs' attitude towards their borrowing levels. Leeds have spread their debt over 25 years, yet in the last 25 years they have spent 8 seasons in the old Second Division. Given the current state of First Division finances after the collapse of ITV Digital, it would be disastrous for any club with Leeds' level of debt to be relegated. Likewise Chelsea, whose profitability would appear to be contingent on participating in European competition, would be in dire straits if they were ever to find themselves playing in the First Division. However, it is unlikely that either will suffer such ignominy, given the quality of their playing squads, and even if they did, their assets – in Leeds case players, in Chelsea's case players and hotels – could be sold.

The biggest threat to both clubs' finances is the same as it is for all Premier League clubs: a dramatic fall in television revenue, either domestic or European. As noted above, reaching the semi-final of the Champions League in 2001 earned Leeds around £18m in television revenue, with another £18m earned from the club's share of the Premier League's deal with BSkyB, while Chelsea's share was £16m. As noted in Chapter 6, there are good reasons to believe that the next Premiership TV contract, due to commence in 2004, will not be worth significantly more than the current one, and could even be worth less. Given that both clubs will have debt to service, as well as high levels of player wages to maintain, failure to qualify for Europe for several seasons, against the backdrop of a less lucrative domestic television deal, would surely have profound consequences on both clubs' finances. Both Ridsdale and Bates know this, which is why they are continuing to try and spend their way to success. Both also know they cannot afford to fail.

The debts of Chelsea and Leeds may the biggest in the English game, but it is wrong to think that those two clubs are in most danger of going bust.

Table 5.1 lists the 20 most indebted clubs at the end of the 2000–01 season. But, as will be shown, there are reasons why some at the top of the list are safer than those near the bottom.

## Table 5.1: England's 20 most indebted clubs at the end of the 2000–01 season

| CLUB | DEBT (£M) |
| --- | --- |
| Chelsea | 66.8 |
| Newcastle United | 65.8 |
| Fulham | 65.4 |
| Coventry City | 42.4 |
| Leeds United | 39.4 |
| Wolverhampton Wanderers | 33.3 |
| Everton | 29.6 |
| Derby County | 27.2 |
| West Ham United | 25.8 |
| Reading | 23.9 |
| Aston Villa | 16.8 |
| Sheffield Wednesday | 16.3 |
| Tottenham Hotspur | 16.2 |
| Southampton | 14.3 |
| Wigan Athletic | 13.1 |
| Huddersfield Town | 9.9 |
| Blackburn Rovers | 9.8 |
| Norwich City | 9.0 |
| Sheffield United | 7.2 |

*Source: Deloitte & Touche,* Annual Review of Football Finance 2002

There are some important provisos that need to be borne in mind when looking at the table. Firstly, the figures are over a year old and much has changed since. Some clubs have been promoted or have had the benefit of one year in the Premier League and reaped the benefits; Blackburn and Fulham fall into this category. Conversely, some clubs have been relegated from the Premier League and their position could well be worse; Coventry, for example, are reported to have over £60m of debt now that they have completed a season in the First Division. Newcastle's and Aston Villa's debts include convertible loan notes issued as part of a deal with NTL. Indeed, apart from the NTL deal, Aston Villa have one of the strongest balance sheets in the Premier League. Some clubs have added to their debt, Chelsea and Leeds, for example; none have actually reduced their debts, but Everton have rescheduled theirs. There are also clubs – such as Middlesbrough – who did not supply sufficient information to Deloitte & Touche for the accountants to be able to calculate their debts so the list has been compiled with information from only 74 out of a possible 92 clubs.

The largest proviso, however, is the presence of clubs that have benefactor funding – that is rich owners who are prepared to bankroll their clubs and try and buy success. Fulham, Wolves, Reading, Blackburn and Wigan fall into this category. Benefactor funding is in fact one of the most traditional ways that football clubs have been funded. Whenever a club got in trouble there always appeared to be a local millionaire around who could bail the club out. It could be argued that benefactor funding has in fact been one of the major contributory factors to the current crisis. Because clubs have always been able to rely on someone to bail them out they have not adopted strict financial controls or best management practice. There are two problems with the benefactor funding model of financing modern football clubs. Firstly there is the issue of what happens when the benefactor runs out of money. Secondly there is the problem that the inflation in football that has taken place over the last ten years means that the benefactors have to be seriously wealthy – two or three million pounds just isn't sufficient to put even a struggling Second Division club on an even keel. In other words, there are no longer enough sufficiently wealthy benefactors to go round.

The case of Mark Goldberg and Crystal Palace is a fine example of what happens when a benefactor runs out of money. When Goldberg bought into Crystal Palace, the club he had supported all his life, in February 1998 he paid £23m to outgoing owner Ron Noades by selling 2.5 million shares in his company MSB International. He retained one million shares in MSB that were worth around £10m, giving him a cushion and the means to invest more in the club if necessary. Palace were heading towards their third relegation from the Premier League and Goldberg appointed Terry Venables, who oversaw Palace's rise from the Third Division to First between 1977 and 1980, leading them to be dubbed 'The team of the '80s'. Goldberg gave Venables funds to try and avoid the increasingly inevitable return to the First Division and Valerina Ismael, Matt Jansen and Sasa Curcic were added to the squad for a total cost of £4.75m. As a director prior to buying the club outright, Goldberg had supplied the funds that bought Attilo Lomabardo and Michele Padovano from Juventus, Neil Emblem and Jamie Smith from Wolves and Itzhik Zohar from Royal Antwerp, and Palace were relegated after spending £13.35m in the transfer market. Because the club subsequently went into administration no details have ever been divulged as to the size of the wage bill it took down to the First Division but it must have been far in excess of the relatively modest £5.3m of the previous year. In January 1998, with over £20m of debt, the administrators were called into the club. Goldberg's ten million MSB shares were worth just £2.35m. Goldberg was reported in the *Daily Telegraph* of 20 February 2002 as having said: 'My MSB shares were my cushion. They are not anymore. They are out of my control.'

That Palace lost so much money so quickly is not entirely due to the wealth gap between the Premier League and the First Division. Indeed, it took some exceptionally bad management by Goldberg to plunge the club into crisis in such a short space of time. Perhaps the worst decision he made was not individual player purchases, but working so hard to secure the services of Terry Venables. Venables demanded and received a fee of £135,000 just for agreeing to enter into talks with Goldberg. He was given a tax-free annual salary of £750,000, the club paid the tax, and a £650,000 house. It was rumoured, but never substantiated, that Venables was to receive a commission on both the sale and purchase of players. Whatever the exact details of the package that Venables negotiated, he claimed to be owed over £7m when the club's creditors were asked to submit claims to the administrators.

It is, of course, doubtful whether Palace would have survived under Goldberg even if his stake in MSB had retained its original £10m value. But the case of Palace is illustrative of the pitfalls of benefactor funding in that it shows what happens when a benefactor is no longer able to benefact. Of recent cases of clubs facing financial difficulties because of a change in the fortunes of a major shareholder, Palace stands out, but there are several other examples. Everton under the chairmanship of Peter Johnson were forced to sell Duncan Ferguson to Newcastle for £7m in November 1998 after Johnson's company Park Foods came under pressure. Bury received substantial investment from fund manager Hugh Eaves but when he was found to have lost £15m of investors' funds, his shareholding had to be sold and the club went into administration.

Football's reliance on wealthy benefactors has been to the game's detriment because it has led to a culture of complacency whereby year-on-year losses and accumulated debts have become acceptable because it has always been expected that another wealthy benefactor will pick up the bill. That may well be the case when debts are under £1m, but there are not enough wealthy benefactors to settle the debts of at least £750m that English clubs have collectively accumulated. As values have increased thanks to football's boom period, so have debts during the subsequent bust. The fact that the business of football has been predicated on the beneficence of a few wealthy individuals lies at the heart of the game's current crisis.

The polarisation of wealth in football has led to a readiness to look to debt as a way of financing the continuing quest for success. The sink-or-swim mentality that motivates Ridsdale's willingness to take on £60m of long-term debt to finance short-term success is prevalent throughout the game. While Ridsdale and Leeds will probably get away with it, because he has embarked on the strategy fully aware of the possible downside and is unafraid to sell players if necessary, there will be many who will not.

## ENDNOTES

[1] www.leedsunited.com
[2] Caspian Group. 1997. Annual report: 1.
[3] www.leedsunited.com
[4] Leeds Sporting plc. 30 June 2000. Preliminary results for the year ended.
[5] Leeds United plc. 8 March 2002. Interim results announcement.
[6] Chelsea Village plc. 2001. Annual report: 7.

# 6. Television

THE COLLAPSE OF ITV DIGITAL AND THE CONSEQUENTIAL PROBLEMS FOR THE FOOTBALL League arising from the failed platform's inability to meet its contractual obligations were hailed as evidence that the football TV rights bubble had finally burst. In fact the evidence first appeared on 18 October 2000 when NTL withdrew its £328m three-year bid to broadcast 44 Premier League matches a season on a pay-per-view basis.

When NTL made its bid four months previously it did so at the same time as BSkyB paid £1.1bn for the rights to broadcast 66 matches a season and ITV paid £183m for the highlights package previously used by the BBC for *Match of the Day*. The total value of the deal to the Premier League was over £1.6bn, a 213 per cent increase on the previous deal. It had looked very much as if English football was in rude financial health, yet four months later, the first questions were being asked about its long-term financial viability.

That NTL had so miscalculated the value of what appeared to be a key component of its programming package should have perhaps raised serious doubts about that company's strategy, but at that time there was no inkling of the scale of the financial black hole into which the New York-listed cable giant was sliding. Eventually the rights were picked up for £100m by a consortium of Sky, ITV and NTL. Other deals, such as the now infamous ITV Digital deal with the Football League, had also been completed.

While the importance of television revenue to football clubs can be, and often is, overstated, there can be no doubt that television money makes up a higher proportion of a modern club's income than ever before. When the

Football League negotiated a joint highlights deal with the BBC and ITV in 1983 it was worth just £28,261 to each of the League's 92 member clubs. As Szymanski and Kuypers in *Winners and Losers: The Business Strategy of Football* point out, that amounted to just 1 per cent of Arsenal's turnover. In 2001 Arsenal reported that 59 per cent of its £62m income came from 'broadcasting and other commercial income'. That figure includes sponsorship and corporate hospitality but Manchester United and Leeds United, who both report TV income separately, said that TV represented 26 per cent and 39.7 per cent respectively of their total income. Television, therefore, is now a major revenue stream for English football clubs, but it is worth remembering that it is a relatively recent one.

The early days of televised football were confined to coverage of the FA Cup final. The first English match to be broadcast live on television was the 1937 FA Cup final between Sunderland and Preston North End, which Sunderland won 3–1. The fact that only an estimated 10,000 viewers tuned in is due more to the limited number of people who had access to the nascent medium than the draw of the tie. In 1950 a million people watched Arsenal beat Liverpool 2–0 and just three years later over ten million watched the famous Matthews final when the legendary Sir Stanley finally won a winner's medal, leading Blackpool to come from behind to beat Bolton 4–3.

The Matthews final showed how football could draw massive audiences but it also illustrated the importance of scheduling to maximise audiences. The 1950 final was played against the backdrop of a full League programme. Although there is no data available to show whether attendances were affected by the rival attraction of the Cup final on TV, the League was sufficiently worried to lodge an objection to the FA. As a result, the 1953 final was played on the last day of the League season and the 1954 final was moved to the weekend after the season had finished. This not only meant that there was no competition for League attendances, it also allowed the Cup final to be watched by all fans.

The Football League's objections to the scheduling of the FA Cup in the early 1950s were a precursor for the relationship between television and the professional game in the mid-1950s when the new ITV commercial channel was keen to offer football in order to attract viewers and advertisers. The League was mainly concerned about the possible negative effect on attendances and for that reason it rejected an offer from the new commercial station of £1,000 per match in 1955. The BBC made an improved offer of £1,500 and this too was rejected, but the principle of competition between broadcasters, the major driver for escalating rights fees in the 1990s, was established.

The clubs were split as to the merits of televised football, with the small clubs, which dominated the League's management committee, opposed and the big clubs in favour. The debate took place against the background of the campaign by the players' union for the abolition of the maximum wage. The maximum was set at £15 per week during the season and £12 per week during the summer and, although the big clubs were in favour of raising the maximum, all clubs opposed its complete abolition. The PFA, however, saw the birth of televised football as a bargaining tool and threatened to boycott games which were televised, a stance that suited the smaller clubs.

In 1960 ITV offered £47,000 for the second half of 26 matches but only Blackpool v. Bolton was shown before the clubs objected that the deal was negotiated on their behalf by the League. ITV managed to get some action the following year when it shared live coverage of the FA Cup final with the BBC for the first time, an arrangement that survives to this day.

When ITV offered the League £15,000 a year for ten years in 1960, the opposition this time came from the big clubs. Although the League's management committee were keen on the deal, Arsenal, Sheffield Wednesday and Tottenham Hotspur threatened legal action to prevent television cameras filming from their grounds unless they could receive more than just an equal share of the fees. An impasse developed with the small clubs in favour of coverage because it meant they would benefit financially and the big clubs opposed as they thought they were being exploited. As a consequence live football stayed off the small screen until 1983.

The main concern for clubs, whether large or small, was the possible effect of live televised matches on attendances. However, developments in broadcast technology in the early 1960s meant that the cost of filming football, and importantly the editing of footage, dropped significantly. This meant that in 1964 the BBC was able to offer £3,000, to be shared by all 92 clubs, for highlights of matches to be shown on Saturday evenings. With an agreement in place not to reveal which matches were to be featured, *Match of the Day* was born with the first programme featuring highlights of Liverpool's 3–2 home victory over Arsenal on 22 August 1964. The programme was an instant success, regularly drawing between 12 and 13 million viewers and soon became an institution. *Match of the Day* helped raise the profile of the game and the exposure was arguably partly responsible for an increase in First Division attendances, but the fees paid by the BBC made very little impact on the bottom line of the biggest clubs. The following year the League was able to charge £60,000 for the highlights package as a bidding war had broken out between the BBC and ITV.

While the FA and the League had successfully managed to leverage something like a realistic price for highlights of both League and FA Cup matches, the 1966 World Cup was another matter. Acting in concert, the broadcasters tabled low bids for a limited number of matches and eventually managed to secure over 50 hours of coverage for a minimal amount. England's victory was watched by an estimated 400 million people worldwide and although the financial benefit to the FA was negligible, the effect on attendances was profound with gates rising continually until the mid-1970s.

One way of minimising the impact of televised live football on attendances is to play the games in isolation when no other matches are scheduled. The scheduling of fixtures has become a central issue of the modern game and one that I will return to in some detail later, but the 1983 deal between the League and the BBC and ITV set a precedent in scheduling matches primarily for the benefit of television. For £4.6m over two years ITV and BBC won the rights to show ten matches a season, provided they were played on Sunday afternoons (ITV) or Friday nights (BBC). Although the price appeared high, the fees were still split equally between all the League's 92 clubs, with each receiving £28,261. The first game to be broadcast was between Tottenham Hotspur and Nottingham Forest on 2 October 1983, a year in which Spurs' total revenue was over £3.5m.

The early 1980s saw significant developments in European television with the introduction of pay television in France and Italy. In 1983 the French station Canal Plus emerged as Europe's first subscription-television service. After an initially poor take-up, subscriber numbers grew rapidly when French League Football was added to the channel's offering. Canal Plus went on to become one of the major players in European media, eventually becoming part of the utilities conglomerate Vivendi. In Italy the three-channel state monopoly was broken in the late 1970s by the emergence of four private commercial stations that were eventually consolidated into Silvio Berlusconi's Mediaset network in 1984. Italy's future prime minister became a major force in televised football from the mid-1980s to the present, consolidating his power within the game with the purchase of AC Milan in 1985. Berlusconi soon saw the value of adding European as well as domestic football to his platform and he has made several attempts to alter the structure of European football to serve the needs of both his club and media interests by the promotion of a European superleague, in 1988 and again in 1998.

The deregulation of European media also spread to Spain and Germany. In Spain the process began in 1983 and by 1988 there were three private stations – Antena 3, Tele 5 and France's Canal Plus – which was also a subscription service. In Germany, media giant Bertelsmann and the smaller Kirch Group formed the satellite service SAT 1, which began broadcasting in 1984.

The new European channels all needed two things, viewers and content, and competition for the former led to an increase in the value of the latter. The value of football as content and a driver of audiences and subscribers was underlined by Rupert Murdoch: 'Sport absolutely overpowers film and everything else in the entertainment genre and football, of all sports, is number one.'[1] Football makes good television for a number of reasons. The very nature of the game, its speed and unpredictability makes it compelling drama and the low-scoring nature of the game means that the result is usually in doubt for most of the 90 minutes' play. Football is televisual in ways other sports such as cricket and ice hockey are not because the size and speed of the ball means that it is easy to follow. Unlike rugby and American football, football has few pauses and breaks in play. Most importantly there is the profile of the sport in Europe; although that has been raised by television, football has always been Europe's number one sport.

One of the effects of the proliferation of private commercial television channels, both terrestrial and satellite, in continental Europe during the 1980s was an increase in incomes for clubs, particularly those that regularly participated in the European competitions, the Champions, UEFA and Cup-Winners' Cups. The lack of a truly competitive market for football television rights and the absence of English clubs from European club competitions after the Heysel disaster of 1985 meant that English clubs found it difficult to compete, in terms of income and concomitantly on the pitch, with their continental rivals when English clubs were re-admitted to Europe in 1990. This is evidenced by the fact that in the ten years prior to the ban, English clubs won ten out of a possible thirty European titles, whereas in the ten years following the lifting of the ban English clubs could achieve only four out of a possible twenty-nine titles (the UEFA Cup and Cup-Winners' Cup being merged in 2000). The decline is even more marked when the Champions Cup, now the Champions League, is looked at in isolation: seven out of the ten pre-ban Champions Cup winners were English, only Manchester United in 1999 won the Champions League after the ban was lifted. While it is true that the absence from European competition had an effect on the way the English game was played, the lack of buying power for the world's best players must also have been a highly significant reason for English clubs' failure to compete as well after the lifting of the ban as they had before it was imposed.

English television underwent its own revolution in 1988 when two satellite stations were launched: British Satellite Broadcasting (BSB) and Sky. Immediately a new element of competition was introduced and football found itself in demand. In June 1998 BSB offered the League an immediate £11m for the first year and a further £25m per year once the platform was up and running. This came as a blow to the BBC and ITV who had managed to keep the fees paid for football relatively low by acting as an informal cartel and were unable to match BSB's bid. ITV, led by Greg Dyke, saw a way of bypassing the League by making an offer to the so-called Big Five of Manchester United, Arsenal, Liverpool, Everton and Tottenham Hotspur, plus five invited clubs, Newcastle United, Nottingham Forest, Aston Villa, Sheffield Wednesday and West Ham. A breakaway ten-club superleague, dubbed the ITV ten, would receive £1m a year each, compared to the £500,000 they were due to receive from the BSB bid, by the simple expedient of breaking away from the League and not sharing any revenue with the other 82 clubs. Although the breakaway eventually floundered, the same principle was to be utilised four years later when the Premier League was formed.

In the face of legal action by the League and opposition from UEFA,

Dyke attended a meeting of all 22 First Division club chairmen where it was agreed to outmanoeuvre the League by changing the revenue distributive system decided on three years previously. In 1985 it had been agreed that the First Division would keep 50 per cent of all League television revenue. The 22 First Division club chairmen now threatened to breakaway from the League unless they were permitted to keep 75 per cent. Dyke has since revealed that he told the Big Five clubs that they would be featured more often than the other First Division clubs and would therefore receive around £1m a year.

In the face of a potential breakaway the entire League accepted Dyke's offer of £52m over four years, but with the new revenue distribution system in place the deal further widened the gap between the First Division clubs and the rest of the League. Dyke was true to his word in that the Big Five were featured more often than the other First Division clubs. Chelsea Chairman Ken Bates later said: 'We saw Arsenal and Liverpool more times than fucking *Coronation Street*'.[2] Because clubs were paid a part of the fee according to the number of appearances, an income gap then began to form within the First Division itself. When the Premier League was eventually formed, the experience of that polarisation led to the smaller First Division clubs insisting on three crucial elements in the political and economic structure of the league: that each club would have one vote and that a two-thirds majority would be required for any changes in structure or revenue distribution. Additionally the revenue distribution system was designed to introduce an equitable element, namely that a third of the revenues would be shared equally between all 22 clubs, while another third was shared according to final league position and the remaining third according to the number of appearances, with every club guaranteed a minimum number of appearances. While the ITV deal of 1988 has been derided for a number of reasons, not least because it increased the wealth gap between rich and poor clubs, there were a number of positives. By showing live football on free-to-air terrestrial television, the profile of the game was raised and as far as spectators were concerned this was a golden age which has gone for ever – an age when they could watch live league football for no cost other than the licence fee. Another positive was that it led to a certain amount of equity in the distribution of television money when the Premier League finally came into being that may not otherwise have been in place. Without that limited amount of equity the current wealth gap within the Premier League would have been even greater than it is.

While ITV secured top-flight League football, BSB and the BBC secured a £6m-a-year joint deal with the FA for FA Cup matches and England home internationals. However, the content that BSB had was not attractive enough to secure sufficient subscribers and the platform soon ran into financial difficulties. Meanwhile, rival Sky was also suffering from slow subscriber take-up. The two platforms merged in November 1990 and British Sky Broadcasting was born. Even the merged company continued to incur huge losses and by June 1991 these had amounted to £750m.

The politics of the formation of the Premier League are dealt with in Chapter 3 but the impact of the economics of the television industry on English football in 1992 cannot be overstated. That BSkyB were prepared to bid £191.5m for the live rights and, as Alan Sugar said at the time, 'blow ITV out of the water', was due to the fact that it had already lost nearly £1bn. Few now doubt that had Sky not won the bidding war, it would have failed to establish itself as England's dominant pay-TV platform. Thus, when the bidding for the Premier League rights was opened, it really was a matter of life and death for Rupert Murdoch's nascent platform.

If securing football content was a matter of life and death for BSkyB, it was almost equally as important for the new Premier League. Indeed the very *raison d'être* of the Premiership was to increase the First Division clubs' share of TV revenue, which many of them predicted was about to rise. The Premier League's first Chief Executive Rick Parry therefore realised that he had to secure a deal that would make the whole exercise worthwhile and, crucially, make it agreeable to at least 14 of the 22 clubs. The fact that when the BSkyB deal was accepted by the League it was by the very minimum majority illustrates how close the deal was to being rejected.

There were two other bidders for the Premier League rights, perhaps the most interesting in the light of recent events being the often overlooked proposal by the Swiss Bank Corporation. The bank proposed a joint venture with the Premier League whereby a dedicated pay-TV football channel would be created with the bank guaranteeing the League a minimum payment upfront and a share of future profits. This idea has recently been resuscitated, but at the time Parry thought the League was not ready for such an ambitious move. The BBC could not afford to bid for the live rights, preferring to go for a highlights package, so it came down to a straight fight between BSkyB and ITV.

According to his evidence to the Restrictive Practices Court in 1999 Parry believed that ITV wanted to show 30 live matches, that is one a week for the duration of the season. Parry also told the court that he thought ITV were not prepared to give a commitment to feature every club, but preferred to concentrate on the bigger clubs. That commitment was included in ITV's final bid of £165m for 5 years for 30 live matches and exclusive highlights. The BBC joined forces with BSkyB, offering to show highlights on Saturday evenings, which helped to allay the fears of some chairmen who were concerned that limiting coverage to pay-TV would have an adverse effect on sponsorship values. It also lifted the combined value of the BBC/BSkyB bid to £214m; £22.5m from the BBC and the remaining £191.5m from BSkyB.

When the Premier League chairmen met on 18 May 1992 they therefore had two bids to choose from. There have been many accounts of that historic meeting, some of them contradictory, but the account of Fynn and Guest in *Out of Time* seems one of the more balanced. Their account tells of how the then Tottenham Hotspur Chairman Alan Sugar telephoned Sky's Sam Chisholm with details of ITV's bid and told him to make another to 'blow them out of the water'. Sugar had a vested interest in the Sky bid as he was the manufacturer of the company's set-top boxes and offered not to vote. However, the other chairmen voted to let him take part and the Sky bid was carried by a 14–6 majority. As it needed two thirds of the votes, Sugar's vote proved decisive.

The 1992 Sky deal was a watershed in the relationship between football and television in England. Because 60 matches were sold, and the season was spread over 30 weeks, it was obvious that 2 matches would have to be played during the week. Because of the UEFA restrictions on when games could be televised, the only available slots were Sundays, and Monday and Tuesday evenings. The deal also allowed Sky to pick what were termed decisive games, those that could have an effect on promotion and relegation issues, and obligated the Premier League to reschedule them accordingly. The 1992 deal therefore gave Sky considerable control over when certain games took place and for that reason alone changed the shape of English football. Over the next ten years the fixture list became a thing of constant flux. In his autobiography Arsenal's Tony Adams spoke of preparing for an FA Cup final and finding it unusual that the game kicked off at 3 p.m. on a Saturday.

The scheduling of matches has become a major issue for attending supporters with some clubs not playing a home game on a Saturday afternoon for several weeks. The problem of arranging fixtures has been complicated in recent years by the proliferation of matches, combined with the international demands on players. FIFA, UEFA and the FA have laid down a set of fixture priorities whereby international matches have the highest priority, European Cup matches second, FA Cup matches third, League Cup matches fourth and at the bottom of the list are Premier League and other competitive fixtures. The reformatting of the Champions League and an increase in the number of clubs that participate in European competitions has meant that the time available for Premier League matches has decreased. The 2000 television deal introduced yet more congestion with pay-per-view games, which demanded their own free window. Finally, the influx of foreign players has meant that tournaments such as the African Cup of Nations and the Confederations Cup are also placing demands on players. It would be unfair to say the 1992 BSkyB Premier League TV deal is responsible for the current crowded fixture list, but it did set a precedent in that for the first time games were scheduled for the benefit of television. Had the ITV deal, which was only for 30 games, been accepted, there would have been more room for manoeuvre later in the 1990s when the number of fixtures increased, but it is unlikely that the Premiership would have limited the number of games to be shown to 30 for long.

One of the most significant consequences of the 1992 deal was a massive increase in the Premier League clubs' incomes. In the last season under the old structure, 1991–92, First Division clubs had a combined income of £162.64m; the following season, the first of the Premiership, income had risen to £201.6m.

The deal was very good for Sky, which had been losing money since its merger with BSB. The first match broadcast under the new deal was Nottingham Forest v. Liverpool, attracting an audience of just 500,000, but subscribers soon started signing up for the £5.99 package and BSkyB was in profit for the first time by 1993.

The 1992 Premier League television deal also contained a clause that obligated BSkyB and the BBC to bid again for the rights when the deal expired in 1996. The Premier League insisted on the clause because it was worried about the possibility of a sudden fall in television income. Under the terms of the deal the broadcasters were obliged to at least match what they had paid in 1992. In the event, the Premier League's fears were unfounded as there were two other bidders for the rights: United News and Media (under the name Jupiter), and Goal, a consortium whose chief partners were Mirror Group newspapers and Carlton Communications. BSkyB wanted to bid for 90 matches a season, three a week, but the Premier League was concerned about overexposure and the effect on attendance, as well as the potential scheduling problems. Eventually Sky bid £670m for 60 matches a season for 4 years. The Goal bid was for a joint venture whereby the Premiership would receive an upfront fee and then a share of the profits from a new venture which would broadcast on a variety of platforms. There was also the prospect of pay-per-view through the emerging cable network, which it was hoped would soon be able to carry a digital signal. The Jupiter bid also involved a joint venture and was similar to the Goal bid, with the crucial difference that it was for 10 years.

The BBC outbid ITV for the highlights package offering £73m for four years compared to £66.5m by ITV. So the status quo was maintained with BSkyB securing the live rights and the BBC the highlights. The total value of the combined deal was £743m compared to £214m in 1992, an increase of 247 per cent.

In the run up to the 1996 deal, the Premier League offered the Football League the opportunity to join forces and sign a joint TV deal, with the Football League receiving 25 per cent of the total revenue. The Football League was divided on the merits of the deal and was further divided when the FA made a counter offer worth £118.5m over five years. Eventually both offers were rejected and a deal worth £125m was signed with BSkyB, a decision that had cost the League £65m by the time the Premier League's deal was signed. Oldham Chairman Ian Stott told the *Daily Telegraph* of 9 December 1995:

> This proves how scandalous and short sighted our decision of last November was. We got it wrong and, who knows, had we negotiated hard we might have got the Premier League to give us 25 per cent of the total pot. But we haven't heard the last of it yet.

Crystal Palace Chairman (at the time) Ron Noades added:

> The biggest drawback is on renewal rights. If we had gone with the
> FA, we were guaranteed 43 per cent of any renewal. The Premier
> League offered us 20 per cent. Both these deals gave us a safety net
> for the future. By going alone we have got £6.5m more in the first
> year, but what happens in five years' time?

What happened was that the Football League was left to sign the doomed
ITV Digital deal in 2000 while just 20 per cent of the Premier League deal
would have yielded £220m a year for four years against the £315m
promised by ITV Digital. It may have been less, but at least it would have
been paid.

By 1996 pay-per-view television had become a reality. That year saw the
first event to be charged for on a single subscription basis when Mike Tyson
fought Frank Bruno and Sky managed to sell the fight to 650,000
subscribers at £9.99 each. Prior to 1996 there had been neither the
technical ability nor the commercial will for the introduction of pay-per-
view. BSkyB was the only company capable of providing PPV, but had
concentrated on building long-term subscriptions. After the Bruno–Tyson
fight, however, the idea of PPV football became more talked about and
people thought its introduction inevitable, nowhere more so than in the
City, where analysts started to make projections about its financial
potential. A report by the consultancy Fletcher Research estimated that
PPV would be worth £450m a season to the Premier League by 2004. Set
against the 1996 TV deal that figure looked like untold riches and the City
responded by supporting the flotations of 1997 in the belief that revenues
from PPV would generate handsome returns for clubs and, in turn,
investors.

The City's enthusiasm for PPV was not, however, shared by all the clubs,
which saw many potential pitfalls with PPV. Primarily there were the issues
of scheduling and the possible adverse effect on attendances. It was
assumed that all matches would be available to buy on an individual basis,
except the 60 matches that made up the BSkyB subscription package.
There was also the issue of how the money generated would be shared. The
larger clubs wanted to be paid more than the smaller ones as they would
be expected to draw more subscribers, but conversely the smaller clubs

wanted the earnings to be shared on a more equitable basis. It was because of these issues that the Premier League rejected BSkyB's 1998 offer to trial PPV. The clubs may have had different reasons for rejecting the proposal, but they were unanimous in doing so.

After the Premier League rejected BSkyB's offer to trial PPV, the broadcaster turned its attention to the Football League and in February 1999 Sunderland's First Division match against Oxford was offered to existing BSkyB subscribers for a fee of £7.95. With a 6 p.m. Saturday kick-off, the distance Sunderland fans would have to travel to attend meant that many felt it preferable to stay in the North East and watch the game in pubs, which had paid £160 to carry the game. Viewing figures were never disclosed but media reports at the time put subscriptions at around 20,000. It was a similar story a few weeks later when Manchester City's visit to Colchester was aired on PPV. Both these matches featured well-supported First Division clubs playing a long way from home at small grounds, so the results of the experiment were less than conclusive in terms of the effect on attendance and likely subscriber numbers. The experiment did, however, show that the technology was up to the task.

The mid-1990s saw another revolution in the British television industry with the continued fragmentation of platforms. Cable had reached one million homes by 1995, the same year in which another terrestrial platform was launched in the shape of Channel 5. Terrestrial digital television had first been demonstrated in 1993 and in 1996 it had become clear that digital television was going to offer a mass of channels, all competing for viewers. Football saw this as an opportunity to address what had been an increasingly nagging doubt about Sky's dominance of the pay-TV market. In 1992 and 1996 Sky had outbid ITV for Premier League rights in more or less a straight fight. The worry for the Premier League was that once Sky had reached a certain number of subscribers it would no longer be prepared to pay more than the absolute minimum for rights, all it would have to do would be to outbid ITV, in the absence of any other serious competition. Another worry was that once Sky had reached a point where subscriber growth was no longer possible, the only way it could increase its own profits would be to drive down the cost of content and pay less for football. However, the arrival of cable and digital meant that there were to be new players in the market for football and values would continue to rise. Just as the boom of the early 1990s was driven by competition between rival platforms, satellite and terrestrial, so, the argument went, the end of the decade would see an increase in the value of rights thanks to the competition between the established platforms and the new ones.

It soon became clear that the Premier League would have to adopt a different method of selling the rights in order to maximise revenues and maintain competition between broadcasters. Sky had already told the Premier League that it would be technically possible for all matches to be shown simultaneously on their satellite digital platform and the launch of ONdigital in 1998 offered even more opportunities. However before the Premier League could decide how it was going to sell its rights from 2001 it had to see off a legal challenge from the Office of Fair Trading.

The Office of Fair Trading initiated proceedings against the Premier League in 1996, but it was not until 1999 that the case was heard by the Restrictive Practices Court. At the heart of the OFT's case was the objection that the Premiership's selling of TV rights collectively was uncompetitive. The OFT argued that by selling the rights collectively the Premier League was denying supporters access to matches, unless they were subscribers to Sky, and that by selling the rights on an exclusive basis it was inhibiting competition between broadcasters. The OFT also claimed that by selling the rights exclusively to one broadcaster, prices were kept artificially high. The Premier League enlisted the support of a wide number of groups including the Football Association and the Football League, as well as supporters' groups. Mr Justice Ferris accepted that the practice of selling the rights collectively and exclusively was indeed 'restrictive', but he ruled that the benefits of the deal for football and consumers meant that an exception could be made. The benefits to football that Mr Justice Ferris identified were that money was redistributed throughout the game and that some of the proceeds of the deal were invested in stadia and spectator facilities. Clearly the case was an important victory for the Premier League as, had it lost, its *raison d'être* would have been undermined. The whole purpose of the Premier League is to enable a collective of clubs to sell its rights and share the proceeds among its members. If the Premier League was unable to sell its TV rights and the clubs were allowed to sell them individually, the League would become even more polarised between large and small clubs than it currently is. Although the Premier League won the case, the 1998 Competition Act meant that subsequent TV deals would also come under regulatory scrutiny. With that in mind, Premier League

Chief Executive Richard Scudamore set about constructing a method of selling the League's TV rights from 2001–02 that would be compliant with English and European Commission competition law, would take advantage of developments in the English broadcast market and deliver increased revenues to the Premiership's member clubs.

Sky launched its digital satellite service in October 1998 and was followed by ONdigital the following month. ONdigital was a consortium whose major shareholders were the independent broadcasters Carlton and Granada. Whereas Sky's digital offerings were available through a satellite dish, ONdigital 's programming was broadcast through a terrestrial signal that only needed a decoder box fitted to a digital television. ONdigital believed that there was customer antipathy towards satellite dishes and that their decoder would prove popular with viewers who had hitherto resisted Sky. In addition to Sky and ONdigital, cable operators NTL and Telewest were also interested in buying Premier League content, as were terrestrial broadcasters the BBC, ITV and Channel 5, who would be interested mainly in highlights. It was clear that with new buyers in the frame for the rights, if the Premier League only offered for sale the same packages as it did in 1996, 66 live games and recorded highlights, there would be more losers than winners. The Premier League therefore adopted a model that would allow all broadcasters a chance to secure some rights by parcelling up the rights in a number of different lots and inviting bids for each. As well as the standard 66 live matches per season, 40 live games were made available for PPV. The highlights package remained as before, but the clubs were allowed to broadcast delayed highlights on their own channels or websites. In order to appease regulatory concerns, the Premier League decided that all packages would run for just three seasons, which would also allow the League to take advantage of any other new developments in the broadcasting industry. In deciding to limit the deals to three years, however, the Premier League increased the clubs' uncertainty over future revenues. Signing players on five-year contracts with only a three-year television deal to help pay their wages is low risk if the next deal is expected to be worth more than the current one. If, as increasingly looks the case, the next deal is worth less, clubs will find themselves with unsustainable wage bills.

As expected, when the deals were announced in June 2000, Sky had secured the rights to the 66 live games per season, but had to pay considerably more than the £670m they paid in 1996. At £1.1bn Sky had pushed the boat out but the figure merely represented how much it thought the package was worth. Sky had signed up 6 million subscribers by 2000 and was turning over £1.8bn. The Premier League remained its main driver of subscriptions and its biggest single content cost. NTL bought the package for the 40 pay-per-view matches, but analysts immediately thought that it had overpaid at £328m. It was estimated that it would need to sell an average of 650,000 subscriptions to each game in order to make a profit – equal to the previous record for a British pay-per-view event, the 1996 Bruno–Tyson fight. ITV outbid the BBC for the delayed highlights, paying £183m, another figure that many thought somewhat high. With a package for overseas rights still to be sold, the Premier League had secured over £1.6bn of revenue over the next three years, fully justifying the hype leading up to the deal. However, there were questions over the long-term viability of the deal, particularly the NTL pay-per-view element. Not only was pay-per-view a relatively unknown concept as far as football was concerned, NTL was buying the third choice of games as Sky had bought the option on the first and second choice for its Sunday and Monday slots. Despite those reservations, there was a profound sense of shock within football when NTL withdrew its bid in November 2000 and a consortium of NTL, Telewest, ITV Digital and Sky bought the rights for £181m. At that figure, it was estimated that each broadcaster would have to sell 73,000 subscriptions to each match, although most broadcasters sold the games en-block and in advance with discounted season tickets.

ONdigital was re-branded as ITV Digital in April 2001 and the previous year it had made its ill-fated £315m three-year bid for 88 Football League matches per season. The nascent digital platform had decided against bidding for the Premier League rights as they were deemed too expensive. The platform had already secured the rights to the Champions League in 1999, but found that it was not a great driver of subscriber growth. The reasons for that are quite simple; UEFA demands that the Wednesday-evening ties are available on free-to-air television in order to guarantee exposure for sponsors so those who are not diehard supporters can possibly be satisfied with following half of a team's group games on free TV. Also the knock-out nature of the tournament means that clubs can be eliminated early on. Quite a few Arsenal supporters subscribed to

ONdigital when the club qualified for the 1999 Champions League but then cancelled their subscription when Arsenal were eliminated after the first group stage. Crucially there is little synergy between the Football League and the Champions League; supporters of teams in the Champions League are not, by definition, supporters of Football League clubs and vice versa. While there may be casual or general supporters who have a passing interest in both the Football League and Champions League, to actually pay for service requires a level of commitment that they do not have. Of all the problems that faced ITV Digital regarding set-top boxes, signal strength and marketing, the mix of its content proved one of the most crucial.

Another reason why ITV Digital found it difficult to capture a large number of subscribers with an offering of some Champions League matches and 88 Football League matches a season was the general increase in the amount of football televised after the 2000 deal had been signed. With a live Premier League Sky game on Monday night, a Champions League fixture on ITV Digital on Tuesday and another on ITV terrestrial on Wednesday, one or possibly two UEFA Cup ties on Thursday, a Football League game on ITV Digital on Friday, a Premier League pay-per-view game on Saturday evening or a Sky game at lunchtime and a plethora of matches on Sunday, the television-viewing football fans could watch live football every day of the week. Unsurprisingly, few did and most chose to forgo the Tuesday-night Champions League fixture and the Friday-night Football League game on ITV Digital. Additionally there were FA Cup, League Cup and England internationals available on Sky, the BBC and ITV Digital and terrestrial. When Sky bought the rights to the Premier League in 1992 there was little other football on television. The European Champions Cup was a knock-out tournament and English clubs were emerging from the post-Heysel ban and were not performing well or being featured on TV. Gradually throughout the 1990s more football was featured on television, but the 2000 deals massively increased English football's television exposure. For the first time even the most committed football fan started to exercise choice and the easiest option was to forgo the ITV Digital offering. Few people outside of South Yorkshire would pay to be able to watch Barnsley v. Sheffield Wednesday, and a good number of those in South Yorkshire who might, would go and see the game at either Bramall Lane or Oakwell. Nor would those outside of South Yorkshire who would pay to watch the game necessarily be willing to pay to see a 'dead game' between Arsenal and Dynamo Kiev in the Champions League.

Much has been and will be written about the demise of ITV Digital as it represents one of the great failures in the history of British broadcasting. At the time of writing it is not known who, if anyone, will buy the platform and whether it will go the way of the last spectacular failure, British Satellite Broadcasting, and be bought out by Sky or someone else. The government's planned analogue switch-off casts a shadow over the future of digital television in the UK and there is a pending court case where the Football League is suing the major shareholders Carlton and Granada for the remaining money due from the contract. So here I will confine myself to the role of English football and its response to the platform's collapse.

Because the Football League was without a chief executive following the defection of Richard Scudamore to the Premier League, the original deal between the Football League and ITV Digital was signed by an ad hoc committee of club chairmen known as the commercial committee. The commercial committee's members were Richard Murray of Charlton, Ipswich Town's David Sheepshanks, Huddersfield Town Chairman Barry Rubery and Leyton Orient's Barry Hearn. When selling TV rights, clubs or governing bodies send potential bidders an invitation to tender. This document lays down exactly what is for sale, with attendant restrictions, and what is expected of the purchaser. So when the Football League was looking for buyers for its television rights from 2001 it sent out an invitation to tender to interested parties. It is beyond doubt that this document categorically stated that any company bidding for the rights would have to prove it had sufficient financial resources to fulfil the contract and that should it default on payments its shareholders would be liable for outstanding monies owed. As the principal shareholders of ITV Digital were Carlton Communications and Granada, those companies would be liable if ITV Digital failed to honour its contract, which is of course what happened.

ITV Digital made its offer to the Football League after receiving an offer to tender and the League's commercial committee signed what is termed a 'heads of agreement'. The heads of agreement is a short contract that spells out the terms of a deal but does not go into the fine legal details – it is rather an agreement to sign a full contract at a later date. The heads of agreement between the League and ITV Digital did not contain a clause that specified parent-company guarantees and this is at the heart of the

League's subsequent dispute with ITV Digital. The League claims that because the invitation to tender asked for bids with parent guarantees, such guarantees were implicit in the heads of agreement. Carlton and Granada argue that the absence of a specific clause referring to parent company guarantees in the heads of agreement means that they are not liable for the debts of ITV Digital. Both sides claim to have legal advice that supports their case and the matter will eventually be settled by the courts.

Of the four members of the Football League's commercial committee that signed the heads of agreement, only Hearn was still with the League when ITV Digital was liquidated. Sheepshanks and Murray were in the Premiership after their clubs had gained promotion and Rubery sold out of Huddersfield Town to concentrate on his business, Pace Micro Technology, which manufactured the set-top boxes for ITV Digital. The League's Commercial Director Brian Phillpots was also a signatory to the heads of agreement and he also left to join the Premier League. Sheepshanks has, of course, since returned to the League with relegated Ipswich so he and Hearn will both be facing the consequences of ITV Digital's collapse as their clubs struggle to make up the shortfall in their finances. The full contract between the two parties was never signed, with Carlton and Granada claiming that they simply never got around to it and the League retrospectively claiming that ITV Digital was deliberately stalling – another one for the courts.

The ITV Digital deal represented the biggest piece of business that the Football League has ever conducted in its 114-year history and one would have thought that it might have been carried out in a more professional manner. It is, though, hard to be too critical of the League as much of what happened was normal business practice and the commercial committee had no indication that the platform was ever in trouble. Indeed there would appear to be a case for saying that the League was misled by ITV Digital over the financial health of the platform. It was reported in the *Soccer Investor Weekly Bulletin* of 3 March 2002 that, at a meeting of League chairmen on 29 November 2001 at Notts County, ITV Digital Chief Executive Stuart Prebble attempted to allay the chairmen's fears about the future of the platform as the media was full of stories speculating that Carlton and Granada were preparing to pull the plug. League Chief Executive Gordon Burns later revealed that Prebble was taped at the meeting: 'Yes, Stuart Prebble was taped when he addressed the chairmen at

Notts County. We tape the meetings routinely. He gave us every reason to believe that Carlton and Granada were fully behind ITV Digital.' After Prebble's words of reassurance, the chairmen could hardly be blamed for expecting to receive the £180m still owed to the League.

Stories first started appearing in the media that ITV Digital was seeking to renegotiate its contract with the League in late January 2002, although no direct contact was made with the League until late March. When ITV Digital did approach the League, its position was clear: either accept £50m over the next two years instead of the £182m owed or the platform will close. Unsurprisingly, the League refused to renegotiate the deal and the platform was placed in administration on 27 March and put up for sale three weeks later.

The consequences of the ITV Digital collapse will be most keenly felt by the First Division clubs. The deal was worth around £3m a year to each First Division club, £600,000 to each Second Division club and £400,000 to each Third Division club. In 2001, the last year of the old Sky contract, the average First Division club had an income of £8.55m so an increase of £3m was hugely significant. At the same time the average wage bill for a First Division club was £8.66m, over £100,000 more than income. It is fair to estimate, therefore, that in 2002, the average wage bill will have increased by around £3m, which is why the lack of the ITV Digital money is so crucial. Many clubs were running at a loss before the ITV Digital collapse and it has made a bad situation even worse. At the time of writing Bradford City have cited the collapse as the reason for going into administration, and Norwich City have cited it as the reason why it is trying to raise around £5m through a share issue to fans. Watford have sacked Gianluca Vialli and other backroom staff and halted building work at Vicarage Road in an attempt to cut costs, and it seems unlikely that those three clubs will be the only victims.

The collapse of ITV Digital also has major ramifications for the Premier League. Apart from the fact that three clubs are relegated from the Premier League to the First Division every season, there is the general effect the collapse will have on the market for the Premier League's TV rights when they are up for sale again in 2004. When the 2001 rights were sold in 2000, the potential bidders included NTL and Telewest. NTL has filed for Chapter 11 bankruptcy in the United States, the American version of administration, and is struggling under the weight of £11bn of debt, while

Telewest has undergone radical restructuring in an attempt to cut costs and is also considering selling out to the US media group Liberty. While ITV and the BBC may still be in a position to bid for the highlights, it seems unlikely that Sky will face the same level of competition as it did in 2000 for the live rights. With no obvious competitor Sky could well be able to bid less than it did in 2000. If Sky has reached a limit on subscriber growth it will need to drive down content costs and the best way to do that would be to pay less for live Premier League matches. Some observers believe that the government's recent Broadcasting Act, which allows foreign companies to own British media companies, will see fresh investment in British broadcasting and the possible takeover of Channel 5. While that may introduce another element of competition to the terrestrial market, it is unlikely to do the same for the pay-TV market, where Sky's dominant position looks unassailable.

If the Premier League is unable to secure a significant increase in TV revenues for its member clubs when the current deal runs out it has two possible options. The first is to set up its own channel and sell the programming to other channels. This option has been discussed before, particularly in 1992 and 1995, but has one major drawback. In order for the clubs to draw immediate income from a Premier League TV channel, which they would need to do to pay player wages, it would need significant outside investment, as offered by the Swiss Bank Corporation in 1992. The problem is that financial institutions are not as enthusiastic as they were about sports broadcasting and if there is still a media recession in 2003, it is unlikely that sufficient funding will be available.

If there is not sufficient backing for a Premier League channel there is always the option that clubs could utilise their own club channels. The first club channel to launch in England was Middlesbrough's Boro TV in 1998 and other clubs soon followed with Manchester United's MUTV being the highest-profile. The alliances formed in the run-up to the 2000 Premier League TV rights auction have led to a number of joint-venture club channels, including Chelsea and Leeds United with Sky. The joint-venture companies set up by Granada with Arsenal and Liverpool were ostensibly for the creation of broadband web portals but could be adapted for digital TV. The main problem that English club channels have encountered has been that the clubs have not had access to their own matches and have only been able to broadcast delayed coverage and highlights. The larger

Premier League clubs have continually pushed for more access to their own games and should the next centrally marketed Premier League TV deal fail to live up to expectations, that pressure will increase. The worry for the Premier League must be that those clubs with their own TV channels will decide that they can earn more from selling coverage of their matches through their own platform than they can through the Premier League. Were that to be the case, then Premier League's days would be numbered.

Football's relationship with television has been in constant flux since the 1950s, when there was hostility towards television, to the 1990s when it looked as if television would take over the game. There are signs that television will become less important financially to clubs over the coming years as broadcasters have neither the inclination nor the means to pay ever-increasing rights fees. Should that prove to be the case, those clubs that have worked hard to build a strong supporter base and developed other alternative revenue streams will be best placed to take advantage of a media downturn. Those clubs who have been complacent and believed that the golden goose of television would continue to lay increasingly valuable eggs will find themselves facing a very uncertain future.

## ENDNOTES

[1] Szymanski, S. and Kuypers, T. 1999. *Winners and Losers: The Business Strategy of Football*. London: Penguin: 62.
[2] Fynn, A. and Guest, L. 1994. *Out of Time*. London: Simon & Schuster: 46.

# 7. Europe

THE CHAMPIONS LEAGUE HAS ASSUMED SUPREME IMPORTANCE FOR CLUBS AT THE TOP OF THE Premier League, as noted in Chapter 5. Manchester United have managed to consolidate their dominance of the English game by regularly competing in the tournament and thereby widening the income gap between themselves and the rest of the Premiership. United earned a profit of £16.9m from their 1999–2000 Champions League campaign, ending in elimination at the quarter-final stage by eventual winners Real Madrid, £8.1m more than the profit the club made after winning the trophy as part of the historic Treble in 1999.

Although United dominated the early days of the Premiership, it took some years before they could become regular European high achievers. After winning the Cup-Winners' Cup in 1990, United were knocked out in the second round the following year and eliminated in the first round of the UEFA Cup by Torpedo Moscow the year after. In 1993 United returned to the European Cup, the last time the competition was a straight knock-out, but lost on away goals in the second round to Galatasaray. In 1994 UEFA re-branded the competition as the Champions League and incorporated a group stage, but United failed to progress beyond it, finishing third to Barcelona and Galatasaray. As runners-up to Blackburn Rovers in the Premiership, United failed to qualify for the Champions League in 1995 and were knocked out of the UEFA Cup by Rotor Volgograd in the first round. The following season, however, saw United start to be more competitive in Europe, progressing beyond the group stage of the Champions League before being eliminated by eventual winners Borussia Dortmund in the semi-finals. Since then United have always progressed beyond the group stages and qualified for the knock-out rounds. Fortunately for United this has coincided with a massive rise in the value of the competition to its competing clubs. How the Champions League became so lucrative and further widened the financial gap between Europe's top clubs and their domestic competitors is a story that perfectly illustrates the economic and political dynamics of European football.

The first European Cup took place in 1955, the year after UEFA was formed. The Football Association was at first sceptical about the competition and forbade the 1955 League champions Chelsea from participating. However the following year Manchester United did take part and reached the semi-finals, as they did in 1958, the year of the Munich disaster. Real Madrid dominated the competition during its early years, winning the first five titles and it was not until 1967 that a British club, Celtic, won the competition. Manchester United followed the next year, beating Benfica at Wembley, thanks to a superb performance by George Best. The late 1970s and early '80s saw English clubs become regular winners with Liverpool winning four times, Nottingham Forest twice and Aston Villa once, from 1977 until 1985, the year English clubs were excluded following the Heysel disaster. As noted in Chapter 4, deregulation of the television industry in continental Europe in the 1980s and the rise of pay-TV saw football as television content rise in value. European Cup football was particularly popular with television audiences as it was played on midweek evenings and gave audiences something entirely different, with foreign clubs and players suddenly in the spotlight. The knock-out format of the competition combined with the outstanding performance of English clubs, Liverpool in particular, made the live midweek coverage a regular feature of British television viewing.

As well as the Champions Cup, the Inter City Fairs Cup and the Cup-Winners' Cup also provoked English interest with English clubs such as Newcastle United, West Ham, Tottenham Hotspur, Arsenal, Manchester City, Ipswich Town and Chelsea all winning various European honours before the post-Heysel exclusion of English clubs.

As the European Cup became more lucrative in terms of television revenue, Europe's top clubs became more dependent on that income. Consequently, they became more concerned about the format of the competition and qualification for it assumed greater importance. As far as the format was concerned, Europe's biggest clubs wanted a league format so they would not be eliminated if they lost just one match. With qualification dependent on domestic League position, failure at home meant an absence of European competition the following season. While these two aspects of European competition would strike most as being eminently fair, many of Europe's top clubs wanted to be guaranteed entry into Europe, and a better chance of competing until the later stages. None more so than Silvio Berlusconi's AC Milan.

Between 1989 and 1995 AC Milan appeared in five European Cup finals, winning three. But the 1997–98 season saw the club finish tenth in Serie A, missing out on an Intertoto Cup place by four points. Berlusconi had invested heavily in the team and the prospect of a Europe-free 1998–99 season became too much to bear. Berlusconi used his considerable influence to attempt to get UEFA to award former European champions a 'wild card' entry straight into the group stages of the Champions League if they failed to qualify through domestic competition. He was helped in his campaign by the fact that the elections for the presidency of FIFA were to be held in June of that year. UEFA President Lennart Johannsson was running against FIFA General Secretary Sepp Blatter. *Gazzetta dello Sport* of 6 June reported that the president of the Italian federation Luciano Nizzola would vote for Johannsson, which would leave the way clear for UEFA executive committee member Antonio Matarrese to succeed Johannsson in the event of the Swede being elected as FIFA president. Matarrese was supportive of Milan's wild card entry and as UEFA president would be in a position to deliver it. In the event, Blatter won the election so the plan proved fruitless and on 27 June UEFA ruled out wild-card entries. However, Berlusconi had been busy with a fall-back strategy.

In July stories in the English and German press began to appear that claimed plans were advanced for the formation of a European Superleague. The Milan-based sports rights agency Media Partners had been working on a plan for some time and reports claimed that talks had taken place with Arsenal, Manchester United and Liverpool. In England, Media Partners retained the public relations company Brunswick, who were undoubtedly behind many of the 'exclusives' that gradually began to put some flesh on their proposals. What emerged was a 36-team competition, with 3 leagues of 12, with end-of-season play-offs to determine the outright winners. Half of the teams would be guaranteed entry judged on their performance over the past five years, while the rest would be selected by their position in their domestic leagues. This would guarantee that the likes of Manchester United, Real Madrid and AC Milan would take part every year, but would also allow small clubs who did well domestically to participate. The Media Partners plan also included a 96-team knock-out competition to replace the UEFA Cup.

There had been several aborted plans for a European Superleague before, but the Media Partners plan had a crucial difference. With the backing of merchant bankers JP Morgan, Media Partners were offering the permanent members ownership of the competition as well as around £20m up front.

The reason why the English clubs were so receptive to Media Partners' plans had less to do with the concept of guaranteed participation than with the amount of money on offer. The Champions League was known to generate around £185m, but UEFA only distributed around £100m to the participating clubs. The rest was distributed to UEFA's 51 member federations and TEAM marketing, the sports rights agency that sold the sponsorship and television rights to the Champions League and was estimated to make around £30m from the competition each year.

Because Manchester United and Arsenal were quoted on the stock exchange, albeit the junior Ofex exchange in Arsenal's case, they had a duty to their shareholders to look at Media Partners' proposals. However, they also had a duty to tell their shareholders that they were doing so, which proved to be a major setback for Media Partners. With the press reports intensifying, United and Arsenal were forced to make statements confirming that talks were taking place, which forced the issue into the open. Media Partners were thus compelled to make their plans public before they had intended to. Those who are critical of the whole concept of clubs being quoted on the stock market should remember that there are benefits for football in the transparency that a listing requires, as was illustrated in the summer of 1998.

UEFA's response to the Superleague threat was to reform its competitions, which many had argued was the whole point of the exercise. Indeed Premier League Chief Executive Peter Leaver said that Media Partners proposals were 'a very useful stick with which to beat UEFA'.[1]

The UEFA congress held in August 1998 agreed to drastic changes to the format of the Champions League and the merging of the UEFA Cup and Cup-Winners' Cup. The main change to the Champions League was the expansion of the group stage of the competition from 24 to 32 teams, playing in 8 groups of 4, with a second group stage of 4 groups of 4. This meant that a winning team would play 17 matches as opposed to 11 under the old format. Extra games mean more money – not only are there more matches to sell to television, but also more home games for which the clubs would keep all the ticket revenue.

While the revamped UEFA competitions did not offer as much financially as the Media Partners plan, they offered significantly more than was previously available and the changes were sufficient to see off the threatened breakaway, for the time being. In giving the third-placed team in the first group stage a place in the UEFA Cup, UEFA was also able to compensate some of the clubs that failed to progress to the second group stage.

Having successfully seen off the challenge of a breakaway European Superleague, UEFA set about making the Champions League even more lucrative for the participating clubs, with notable success. With more games to sell to television, UEFA and its marketing partner TEAM were helped by developments in the European media industry. In England, the emergence of digital pay-TV, in the shape of ONdigital, introduced a new element of competition in the battle for rights. Similarly in Germany, Rupert Murdoch used the small pay channel TM3 to bid for the rights. With sponsorship and TV rights values higher than ever before, UEFA was able to raise £670m for the 2000–01 season, with £490m distributed to participating clubs. Each of the 32 participating clubs received £730,000 just for turning up and then £335,000 for each group stage win and £165,000 for each draw. Quarter-finalists received bonuses of £2.65m, while the four semi-finalists each received £3.35m. Bayern Munich earned a £15m bonus for winning the final in Milan, bringing the German club's Champions League earnings to £47m. Runners up Valencia received a £4m bonus to bring their earnings from the tournament to £27.5m. Those figures do not include home-gate money, of which all participating clubs keep 100 per cent.

The 1998 breakaway European Superleague saga showed Europe's top clubs just how much they could achieve by threatening to go it alone and they decided to keep up the pressure on UEFA by forming their own pressure group, G14. The group was formed in November 1999 and legally constituted in June 2000. The group comprised former European Champions AC Milan, Bayern Munich, Olympique Marseille, Porto, Real Madrid, Ajax Amsterdam, Borussia Dortmund, Barcelona, Inter Milan, Juventus, Liverpool, Manchester United, Paris St Germain and PSV Eindhoven. The initial membership was selected according to strict sporting criteria in that the clubs had to have won the European Cup. A voting structure was formulated whereby all founding member clubs had three votes and all clubs that subsequently joined had one vote each. Clubs were given an extra two votes for each European Cup title won and one for each UEFA or Cup-Winners' Cup title, limited to a maximum of 16 votes. This meant that Real Madrid had the maximum 16 votes, while Manchester United had just 8 and Porto 5. However, constitutional matters, such as expansion of the group, would need the unanimous support of all member clubs. It was immediately noticed that some clubs were conspicuous by their absence. Italy was represented by three of its big seven, with Lazio, Roma, Parma and Fiorentina excluded. In England Arsenal were missing, while Spain's Deportivo la Coruna and Valencia, both of whom were threatening the traditional Barcelona–Real Madrid hegemony, were also absent. True, none of the excluded clubs had won a European Cup, but they were still major forces in European football. Previous European Cup winners who were not invited to join were Celtic, Nottingham Forest, Aston Villa, Hamburg, Steaua Bucharest and Red Star Belgrade.

In announcing the legal foundation of G14, its Chairman, Real Madrid President Lorenzo Sanz, said:

> This is a very important day for football. Our idea is to provide continuity to the work we have undertaken up to now and increase our contacts with FIFA and UEFA in the defence of the interests of football. Our new association will benefit the interests of the clubs and football itself.[2]

The aims of G14 were expressed in the founding agreement thus:

- To foster co-operation and unity among member clubs.
- To promote co-operation with FIFA, UEFA or other sports organisations and clubs.

- To contribute to decisions on the format, organisation, administration and commercial interests of international club football.
- To promote the objectives of member clubs and to jointly assess all matters of common interest.
- To support economic development to the benefit of G14 members.[3]

While the founding principles of G14 seem innocuous enough, it is obvious that the main reason for its existence is to promote the interests of Europe's top clubs, even if that is to the detriment of smaller clubs. The group is hindered in this objective by the limited size of its membership. G14's main bargaining chip is the implicit threat of a breakaway: however, since 1999 that threat has become increasingly empty. With only 14 members and the absentees listed above, G14 cannot offer a viable alternative to the Champions League. Although the group has been successful in forcing some changes in the format of UEFA's competitions and the distribution of its income, its other achievements are limited. Some G14 clubs have recognised the group's weakness and sought to have the membership increased, but met with opposition from two clubs: Barcelona and Marseille. Both objected for domestic reasons. Marseille were under-performing in the French league and saw their G14 membership as a status symbol within French football. Likewise, Barcelona objected to Valencia or Deportivo being admitted because that would raise their status in Spain at a time when Barcelona were under-performing in La Liga. The intransigence of Barcelona and Marseille has caused a certain amount of friction within the group and has led to some clubs questioning the worth of membership.

An English newspaper recently claimed in an interview with G14's Chief Executive Thomas Kurth that 'what G14 wants, G14 gets'. Nothing, however, could be further from the truth. In that interview Kurth said the clubs wanted guaranteed entry into the Champions League, but Real Madrid President Florentino Perez was quick to deny that the issue was on G14's agenda. Because of G14's size and its inability to expand it has been largely marginalised as far as UEFA is concerned. Far from G14 getting what it wants, it seems unable to agree exactly what it is that it wants. The issue of the format of the Champions League is a case in point.

On 20 March 2002, Juventus beat Arsenal at the Stadio D'Alpi in the last game of the Champions League second group stage in front of a crowd of only 8,562 – clearly something was wrong with the format of Europe's premier club competition. True, the match drew a television audience of 5.8m on ITV1, but the stupefying atmosphere in which the match was played was epitomised by the sound of a police dog barking throughout the second half, making more noise than the crowd. The poor turnout did not occur in isolation either; only 4,526 watched Bayer Leverkusen's visit the previous November, nor was falling interest a solely Italian phenomenon. In the first group stage of Bayern Munich's triumphant 2001–02 Champions League campaign, attendances were down by 33 per cent on the previous year to an average of 24,000, compared to a Bundesliga average of 48,471. Back in 1999 a first-round match against Helsingborgs drew only 20,000. Even Real Madrid have found European football less of a draw than La Liga with an average Champions League attendance of 58,164, compared to 64,475 for league games. When Real Madrid beat Molde in a first-round group game in November 1999, only 9,000 supporters watched at the Bernebau – Real's lowest attendance in any competition since the 1960s. It was the same story with TV ratings: the total live audience in the top six markets (Germany, France, England, Italy, Spain and Holland) was 857 million for the 1999–2000 season, but only 750 million the following season and the total live audience per week fell to 44 million from 50 million. This fall occurred at a time when there was more coverage, with 3,958 hours in 2000–01, compared to 2,375 the previous season. Research by Mediametrie/Eurodata showed that in Italy by 2001 Champions League viewing had steadily fallen by 4.6 per cent since the 1997–98 season. In France viewing had fallen by 3.7 per cent while in England it had fallen by 6 per cent since the high of Manchester United's 1999 victory.

That the most animated member of the Turin audience for the Juventus v. Arsenal match cited above was a police dog was due in part to the fact that, to all intents and purposes, the match appeared to be a dead game. Because it was the last match day of the group, Arsenal needed to win in the D'Alpi and Bayer Leverkusen to win away against Deportivo La Coruna – which seemed improbable given previous results – for Arsenal to qualify. As is often the way, Leverkusen achieved the seemingly impossible, winning 3–1, while Arsenal lost 1–0. But the point is that any league format will inevitably produce some games towards the end of the competition that are meaningless. UEFA tried to reduce the possibility of dead games by allowing the third-placed team in the first group stage of the Champions League entry into the UEFA Cup but the effect was to so devalue the latter tournament that it was dropped after two seasons.

Another factor that lessened the appeal of the Champions League, especially in the latter stages, was the competition's domination by teams from the same country, particularly Spain and England. Of the eight quarter-finalists in 2000–01, three were English (Leeds United, Manchester United and Arsenal), and three were Spanish (Deportivo, Valencia and Real Madrid), with Galatasaray and Bayern Munich making up the numbers. While that was undoubtedly good news for English and Spanish fans, it did little to entice viewers in Italy, France and Holland. Sponsors like the Champions League because it gives them exposure across Europe. When 75 per cent of competitors come from just 2 of 51 possible markets it seriously undermines the marketing strategy which underpins their investment.

Throughout the summer of 2001, there were various voices of dissatisfaction with the extended format. UEFA's Professional Football and Marketing Director Lars-Christer Olsson told the Sportbusiness 2001 conference that he thought there were too many matches and that: 'We will be looking to reformat the Champions League to maintain interest in different markets.' Similar concerns were raised by Bayern Munich President Franz Beckenbauer: 'Thirteen games instead of seventeen would be enough. After the first group stage we should go straight into the knock-out phase with the round of eight.'

With powerful voices within UEFA and G14 calling for reform it looked as if the format of the Champions League would be changed once more but when G14 met in Monaco in August 2001 with the issue of the Champions League on the agenda, the group's inertia kicked in. While it is not known exactly which clubs voted for expansion of the Champions League and which voted for reduction, it is safe to assume that Bayern Munich and Manchester United were in favour of fewer matches, based on what Bayern had said publicly and Manchester United's consistent complaints about the size of the Premier League and an overcrowded domestic fixture list. Real Madrid and Juventus were thought to be in favour of more games, despite there being no evidence that their supporters had an appetite for them. In any event, the result of the Monaco meeting was deadlock. After hours of deliberation G14 could only agree on a compromise: to keep things as they were. Thus the group's message to UEFA was to keep the current format, at least until 2003. With the group encompassing such diverse opinions and interests as those of Porto, Ajax, Real Madrid and Juventus, it was hardly surprising that no change was the best that they could agree on. Thus on the fundamentally important issue of the declining interest in the Champions League, G14 came up with a solution that none, or very few, of the clubs actually wanted.

With the failure of the Monaco meeting to produce a coherent position on the Champions League and agree on G14's expansion, a few members were left questioning the usefulness of the group. True, other issues such as the club-versus-country debate and the international transfer rules found G14 united, but then its position on these matters is the same as most of Europe's top division clubs. When G14 says that it speaks for all of football, there is an element of truth in that the only time it is able to speak at all is when it adopts uncontroversial positions that all football, or rather all professional clubs, would also agree with.

There is a temptation to write off G14 as ineffective and almost irrelevant but there is one issue on which it could prove decisive: salary caps. The massive increase in player wages is a Europe-wide phenomenon and needs a transnational response. The G14 clubs have been responsible for driving up player wages for several years. The highest-paid players of recent years – Rivaldo (Barcelona), Del Piero (Juventus), Ronaldo (Inter Milan), Figo and Zidane (Real Madrid) and Beckham (Manchester United) – have all been employed by G14 members. The Italian clubs were the first to feel the pinch as they failed to compete as effectively in the Champions League as they had done in the past. They started to amass massive debts and in November 2001 a task force led by AC Milan Chief Executive Adriano Galliani was set up to look at imposing a limit on Serie A wages. Real Madrid's financial controller Javier Porquera said in March 2002 that G14 could limit its member clubs to spending 65 per cent of turnover. The issue of salary caps will be further examined in Chapter 10, but for the moment it is worth making a couple of observations on G14's attitude towards the issue. If player wages are limited to a percentage of turnover across all of football, then the richest are able to maintain their superiority. If, on the other hand, the G14 clubs act unilaterally and impose an informal limit then there is an opportunity for so-called lesser clubs to catch up. A unilateral G14 wage cap would, however, remove the main driver for wage inflation as the phenomenon is driven from the top down. At the time of writing it is not known which, if either, of the options G14 will opt for, although the former would appear to be true to type. That said, given G14's record on important issues, it is unlikely that a consensus will be reached and G14 will probably sit on the fence.

At the heart of G14's dissatisfaction with UEFA are the issues raised by its centralised marketing of the Champions League. Firstly there is the fact that in the 2000–01 season £490m was distributed to the clubs, but £180m wasn't. There was TEAM's commission for marketing the tournament and the money that UEFA distributed to all 51 of its member federations. Additionally there were payments totalling £37m aid for the development of youth football. Naturally Europe's top clubs object to seeing what they perceive as money that they raise being given away, no matter how worthy the causes. Clubs such as Manchester United and Real Madrid rightly believe that they could earn more if they sold the rights to their games themselves, as is the practice in the UEFA Cup. They also complain that they have no ownership of highlights rights which they could use on their own TV channels or websites. At Manchester United's interim results presentation in the City in September 2001 Chief Executive Peter Kenyon complained that United was unable to show the dramatic late goals that saw the club win its historic Treble in Barcelona in 1999 because UEFA owned the rights. He thought it absurd that the rights to one of the finest moments in the club's history were owned by UEFA and suggested that he believed that would change when the current Champions League deals expire in 2003.

UEFA's other European club competition, the UEFA Cup, is not centrally marketed like the Champions League. This is because it is a straight knock-out competition, a format that doesn't easily lend itself to being sold as a whole. Sponsors and broadcasters would be unwilling to commit substantial investment for a competition that can be of variable quality. The main problem is the number of matches in the early stages, all played on a Thursday night. This means that interest can be significantly diffused as people cannot watch more than one game at a time. In the early rounds it is not uncommon to see several clubs from the same country competing simultaneously, indeed in the third round of the 2000–01 competition there were seven German clubs in the competition once Hamburg and Leverkusen were parachuted in after finishing third in their Champions League groups. So clubs in the UEFA Cup are able to sell the television and sponsorship rights to their matches themselves. For English clubs the going rate for television rights is around £1.5m per round but the actual amount is dependent on the opposition and also which other clubs they are competing with. When Leicester made their European debut in 1997 they drew Atletico Madrid and could reasonably have expected a decent payday. However, the same night that they were playing at home (clubs are only able to sell the rights to their home games), Liverpool were playing Celtic, while Arsenal and Aston Villa played PAOK Thessalonica and Bordeaux respectively. Clearly Leicester's match had the least appeal and the club was unable to find an English broadcaster who was prepared to pay a decent fee. Fortunately for Leicester, Madrid are a hugely popular team in Spain and they were able to sell the rights to a Spanish broadcaster for £250,000. Had they been drawn against an Eastern European team they would have struggled to make any profit at all from the match.

Whether or not a club actually makes any money out of the UEFA Cup has largely been a matter of chance. Liverpool may have made around £12m when they won it last in 2001, but Chelsea were eliminated in the first round by St Galen in the same competition. This uncertainty is one of the factors that has led UEFA, with the support of the clubs, to consider introducing group stages to the competition. Leeds United and Aston Villa have both told the author that they are in favour of the change but, crucially, they would still prefer to be able to market the rights to group-stage matches themselves.

There is another reason why UEFA are keen to introduce a group stage to the UEFA Cup, and as in the case of reforming the Champions League, it is the threat of a breakaway competition. In the autumn of 1999 newspapers reported that the two Glasgow clubs, Celtic and Rangers, were considering joining a breakaway Atlantic League. The plan was that the Old Firm would join with clubs from other countries that also operated in small TV markets – Holland's PSV Eindhoven, Ajax and Feyenoord; Belgium's Anderlecht and FC Bruge; Portugal's Benfica, Porto and Sporting Lisbon; and AIK Stockholm and IFK Gothenburg from Sweden – and play in a midweek league. The financial reasoning was simple; Scotland has a population of five million, which severely limits the potential for television income. If the Old Firm competed in an Atlantic League, the potential audience would be around 50 million, with a concomitant increase in the value of television rights.

UEFA's response to a threatened breakaway Atlantic League was similar to its response to the Media Partners plan: on the one hand it dismissed the idea, while on the other it looked at the format of its competitions to see if it could address some of the issues behind the plan. The introduction of group stages for the UEFA Cup was deemed to be a solution. At the time of writing it looks as if the favoured format would be for an 80-team qualifying knock-out phase, followed by a group stage of eight groups of five. The crucial difference between the proposed UEFA Cup group stages and those of the Champions League would be that clubs would not play each other twice, home and away, but would play two matches at home and two away, so each group would only feature four match days rather than eight. The 16 group winners and runners-up would then go into a knock-out phase, with all matches, except the final, played over two legs.

UEFA estimates that a UEFA Cup reformatted along the lines above would generate double the current total revenues of £103m. UEFA wants the competition to be centrally marketed like the Champions League and it would appear that it has the broad support of the clubs in this matter as revenues from the current format are so uncertain. Participation in the group stage would at least guarantee the clubs four matches, two of them at home. By only having 20 matches in the group stages the possibility of dead games is diminished, but not eliminated. UEFA's estimate of double the revenue would appear somewhat optimistic as there would in fact be 189 matches from the first round onwards, compared to 205 under the current format. With matches played in two simultaneous groups on Thursday evening, direct competition between two teams from the same country can be reduced; however, if four clubs from the same country are involved in the group phase, at least two will be playing simultaneously. Admittedly, there are enough channels available for it to be possible for all matches to be shown, but audiences will obviously suffer.

Whether or not the reformatted UEFA Cup will deliver sufficient income to see off an Atlantic League remains to be seen, although it has to be said that the Old Firm has recently turned its attention towards joining either the English Premier League or First Division, diminishing the possibility of the other Atlantic League clubs setting up an alternative competition. The desire of the Old Firm to play anywhere except Scotland will have an increasing influence on the shape of European and English football competitions. It has already contributed to the reformatting of the UEFA Cup, has been seriously considered by a number of First Division clubs leading to discussions of a Phoenix League and is attractive to a number of powerful Premier League chairmen. The obstacles that the Old Firm would have to overcome to move outside of Scotland are manifold, but not insurmountable and the merits of their case warrant serious discussion.

The Old Firm use two basic arguments to justify why they should play outside of Scotland, either in England or some kind of European league, both of which point to their relative underperformance in the UEFA Cup and the Champions League. In 2002 Celtic reached the group phase of the Champions League for the first time where they finished third behind Juventus and Porto. Celtic then went into the UEFA Cup where they were immediately knocked out by Valencia. That was Celtic's best performance since they reached the semi-final of the Champions Cup in 1974, although they were knocked out of the same competition in the quarter-final by Real Madrid in 1980. In recent years Celtic have suffered second-round UEFA Cup defeats by Lyon and Bordeaux in 2000 and 2001 and have failed to progress beyond the second round proper in either the UEFA Cup or Cup-Winners' Cup since being knocked out of the UEFA Cup by Nottingham Forest in 1984. Rangers reached the fourth round of the 2002 UEFA Cup where they were knocked out by the eventual winners Feyenoord. The two seasons prior to that saw the club knocked out of the first-round group stage of the Champions League and on both occasions Rangers were then knocked out of the UEFA Cup by German opposition; Kaiserslautern in 2001 and Borussia Dortmund in 2000. Victories over the likes of Leeds United in the Champions League in 1992 have been tempered by defeats in qualification for the group stage in 1994 by Levski Sofia. The Old Firm like to blame this perceived underperformance on two things. Firstly it is argued that because they operate in a relatively small television market they are unable to buy European-quality players. Celtic may earn £2.5m from domestic television as winners of the Scottish Premier League, yet the club finishing bottom of the English Premier League earns at least £10m. Secondly, they argue that because they so dominate Scottish football, both financially and in terms of honours (due to their greater financial strength), they do not face the required level of domestic football competition to be able to compete with Europe's best. Both these arguments are somewhat disingenuous.

In recent years teams such as Sturm Graz from Austria, Slavia Prague from the Czech Republic and Rosenborg from Norway have all managed to reach the second group phase of the Champions League while the Old Firm has struggled. Sturm Graz are a good example of a club that operates in a small television market who have punched above their weight on the European stage. In the 1999–2000 season Graz qualified for the Champions League group stage by beating Servette over two legs and of their total revenue of £6.3m, a substantial amount came from that campaign. The following year the club did even better, reaching the second group stage, and 2000–01 turnover will exceed £10m. While there may be some criticism that clubs from minor television markets always have to pre-qualify for the Champions League proper, irrespective of how they perform year on year, even the qualifying matches can be lucrative at that level as the clubs keep all the home gate receipts and television income.

All three clubs cited above earn less from domestic television than either of the Old Firm clubs, as does Dynamo Kiev, a regular high achiever in the Champions League. These clubs manage to achieve relative European success without spending huge amounts in the international transfer market and operate in domestic leagues that are no more competitive than the Scottish. The Old Firm's complaint that low domestic television revenue is a reason why they are unable to compete in Europe is baseless. In 2000–01 Rangers earned £51.7m and were the 15th richest club in the world, according to Deloitte & Touche, while Celtic earned £38.6m and were the 22nd wealthiest club. In the previous year Rosenborg earned £9.7m, of which £3.2m came from the club's Champions League campaign, where they reached the second group phase. Rosenborg dominated Norwegian football throughout the 1990s, winning eight league titles, so it would not appear as if the Norwegian league is any more competitive than the Scottish. How Rosenborg can consistently perform well in Europe while the Old Firm struggle despite considerably greater resources, remains a mystery. It could be worth noting, however, that Celtic's finest moment was winning the European Cup in Lisbon in 1967 against Inter Milan when all the Celtic side were born within five miles of Celtic Park. The Old Firm spend a lot of money attempting to buy

European success, importing players from all over the world, but perhaps the key to success lies closer to home.

The Old Firm's complaint that the level of domestic competition that they face week in and week out ill prepares them for European competition has a simple, if unpalatable, solution. Scottish football is uncompetitive because two teams attract by far the largest crowds and earn significantly more income than the rest of the league. The league could become more competitive if mechanisms for a more equitable method of revenue distribution were adopted. Unsurprisingly, the Old Firm have shown no enthusiasm for such changes, preferring to concentrate their efforts in trying to persuade England and Europe to change their competitive structures to satisfy their ambitions. Thankfully, neither the English nor the European authorities look likely to accommodate the Old Firm so perhaps Rangers and Celtic will start looking to solve their perceived problem themselves, rather than expect the rest of football to solve it for them.

There is a perceptible shift in the economic balance of power in European football that has seen English clubs at last able to compete with their Spanish and Italian counterparts in terms of player-purchasing power. Until last year when Manchester United paid a total of £54.6m for three players – Van Nistelrooy, Veron and Forlan – the annual Deloitte & Touche list of the world's richest clubs was greeted with a certain amount of scepticism – United were always at the top of the list, yet never seemed able to match the big Italian and Spanish clubs in transfer spending. It was not just Manchester United's position at the top of the list that appeared anomalous. The 2001 Deloitte & Touche Rich List featured seven English clubs in the top twenty (Manchester United, Chelsea, Arsenal, Leeds United, Tottenham Hotspur, Liverpool and Newcastle United) and seven Italian clubs (AC Milan, Lazio, AS Roma, Inter Milan, Juventus, Fiorentina and Parma). Barcelona and Real Madrid represented Spain, while German clubs Bayern Munich and Borussia Dortmund also featured. Yet 12 of the world's most expensive transfers have been to Italian clubs, five have been to Spanish clubs and only two to English clubs. The reason for this apparent anomaly is in the difference in what is known as the business mix in English and continental clubs. Although Manchester United, with a turnover of £117m in 2000, had the highest total earnings of any club in the world, that income was from a variety of sources; £36.6m from gate receipts, £30m from television, £18m from sponsorship and advertising and £23m from merchandising. The same year AC Milan earned a total of £89.7m, of which just £13.5m was derived from gate receipts and only £2.8m from merchandising. However, AC Milan's television income was £52.5m and sponsorship earned the club £13.3m. Television and sponsorship income yields high profit margins as it incurs few costs to the club. Conversely, gate money and merchandising sales incur associated overheads – staff for gate receipts and product costs for merchandising – and produce lower profit margins. Therefore the £52.5m that Milan earned from television could all be spent on transfers and player wages, while a significant part of the £59m that Manchester United earned from gate receipts and merchandising would have to be allocated to overheads. Italian and Spanish clubs have traditionally earned significantly more than English clubs from high-margin revenue streams such as sponsorship and television and that is why they have been able to outspend English clubs in the international transfer market, but that looks set to change. On the one hand English clubs are set to enjoy, for the next couple of years at least, significantly higher television earnings thanks to the latest television deal. On the other hand, the Italian and Spanish television industries are struggling to justify the huge fees they have paid for football TV rights in terms of subscribers and viewers. In Italy the massive amounts paid to clubs by the two competing pay-TV channels, Stream and Telepui, have caused problems for both and it is now proposed that the platforms merge. Just as competition between broadcasters has driven up the value of football rights, consolidation will surely bring those values down again.

Italian and Spanish clubs have also managed to finance high transfer fees and player wages through accumulating massive levels of debt compared to their English counterparts. However, that also looks set to change. The motivation for UEFA's licensing scheme is to create a level playing field throughout Europe. It has been considered unfair that Italian and Spanish clubs have been able to buy success with money they do not actually have, while clubs in France and Germany, where domestic club licensing schemes are in place, have to balance their books at the end of each season or suffer sanctions, including relegation, from their governing bodies. Although UEFA's licensing scheme is not scheduled to take effect until 2004, some continental clubs are already trying to reduce their debt levels so as to be compliant. Real Madrid for example have sold their training ground as part of a programme initiated by club President

Florentino Perez to wipe out the club's reported £250m of debt. However, some continental clubs are already paying the price for years of financial irresponsibility. Fiorentina, for example, were the world's 14th richest club in 2000, but were relegated from Serie A in a state of near bankruptcy in 2002, having racked up debts of around £100m. As football's financial crisis spreads throughout Europe, it would seem that there may well be more high-profile casualties like Fiorentina in the not too distant future.

UEFA's efforts to introduce a sense of financial responsibility to the higher levels of the European game could be a case of too little too late, or closing the stable door after the horse has bolted. Similarly, the moves by G14 to halt the escalation in player wages are confined to a narrow group of already well-run clubs. If English football is in crisis, the same can be said of the game in the rest of Europe. Just as the English game needs radical restructuring and reform at all levels, so does the rest of European football. Whether there is the will for such reform and restructuring is questionable, but it needs to happen if the European game is to survive.

## ENDNOTES

[1] *Soccer Investor* (6), 1998.
[2] Reuters, 9 June 2000.
[3] G14 Funding Statement, July 2000.

# 8. The FA

AFTER THE 1996 EUROPEAN CHAMPIONSHIP FINAL AT WEMBLEY THE TOURNAMENT'S DIRECTOR Glen Kirton, the FA's Chief Executive Graham Kelly and its Director of Public Affairs David Davies met and decided that the FA should bid to host the 2006 World Cup finals. They were unaware, so they claimed, that FA Chairman Sir Bert Millichip had previously reached a 'gentleman's agreement' with the German FA that the FA would support the German 2006 bid in return for their support for England's bid to host Euro '96. So started the ill-fated campaign that was to dominate the FA's agenda for the following four years and lead to an overhaul of the Association's structure and personnel. Every subsequent policy decision was made with England's bid as the foremost consideration; from the decision to rebuild Wembley as the centrepiece of the bid to the choice of Malta, whose Federation President Josef Misfud was a FIFA executive member, as opponents for England's final warm-up friendly before the 1998 World Cup in France. The latter is now just seen as an embarrassing footnote in the history of the England team, albeit one that saw Alan Shearer pick up an injury that ruled him out of England's early matches at France '98. The former remains as a testimony to the governing body's vanity and incompetence.

The Football Association was formed in 1863 and was the world's first football governing body, hence the absence of a national prefix. It formulated the rules of the game as it is played worldwide and retains a privileged role regarding the laws of the game through membership of FIFA's International Football Association Board, the body responsible for changes to the game's rules. The FA enjoyed a monopoly of power for 25 years before the formation of the Football League in 1888, which initiated a power struggle that would dog the English game up to the present.

As the world's first football governing body, the FA did not have a model on which to base itself. Then, with the formation of the Football League the role of the FA became somewhat ambiguous – it retained the role of being the ultimate authority on sporting matters, but on commercial matters ceded power to the League. There is more than a little irony in the current commercialism of the FA when compared to its opposition to professionalism in the 1880s. It is now, however, a multi-million-pound business as well as a governing body and this dual identity is crucial to understanding why it fails as both. The FA may claim, as Chief Executive Adam Crozier did in the foreword to the 2001 FA handbook, that its purpose is to 'lead the development of the game and to increase the opportunities that football has to put something back into society as a whole', but such lofty ideals cost money and as long as the FA is focused on making money, its role as a governing body will be compromised.

The transition of the FA from a purely sporting association – concerned only with the governance, regulation and promotion of the game – into a high-profile company that turns over millions has occurred mainly over the last ten years, during the football boom. Its transition has also occurred at a time when English football has gained a higher political profile, of which the government's involvement in the Wembley project is just one example. Another is the government's Football Task Force, which will be dealt with in the final chapter.

Prior to the formation of the Premier League the Thatcher government was generally perceived as being hostile towards football, and not without good reason. However, while its reaction to the tragedies at Bradford, Heysel and Hillsborough was highly prescriptive – identity cards, the removal of the terraces and the conversion of stadia to all-seater – it did also provide some funding for its implementation through the support of the Football Trust funded by a levy on the football pools. The Taylor Report and its implementation was a clear example of the government of the day taking over responsibility for aspects of the governance and regulation of the game that hitherto had been left to the Football Association. The relationship between football and government changed significantly when John Major succeeded Thatcher as Prime Minister in 1990. Whereas Thatcher had barely concealed her loathing for the game and the people who supported it, Major was a sports fan and a Chelsea supporter to boot. As well as directing around £200m of public money through the reduction in the pools levy via the Football Trust into football for the implementation of the Taylor Report, the Major government threw its weight behind England's 2006 World Cup bid. Tony Blair's 1997 Government inherited the World Cup bid and the new Wembley stadium project and, with the appointment of Chelsea-supporting Tony Banks as Sports Minister, became actively involved in supporting the bid.

Despite all the words written about the 2006 World Cup bid, no satisfactory reason was ever given as to why England, having hosted the World Cup finals 40 years previously, should be awarded the tournament. All the publicity material produced by the FA claimed that England was ready; England had some of the world's best stadia and had proved that it had the necessary infrastructure at Euro '96. A 1998 promotional video calls England the 'home of the game' and the 'home of the world's oldest football competition' as well as showing how the new Wembley would look when it was completed. The FA's constant claim, however well justified, that England was the home of the game was viewed in some parts of the world as arrogance born out of colonialism. The reference to the FA Cup as the world's oldest football competition seemed unfortunate as the FA encouraged Manchester United to withdraw from the competition in 2000, in order that they could compete in the World Club Championship (the newest football competition in the world?) and thus carry favour with FIFA and help the 2006 bid, an action that seriously undermined the FA Cup's credibility. Wembley remains in a state of dereliction, eight years after the decision was made to rebuild it.

The competing bids from South Africa and Germany at least had some political rationale behind them. In South Africa's case it was seen as a way to reintegrate the country into the rest of the sporting world after years of apartheid-induced exile. With Germany it was seen as part of the process of reunification that followed the collapse of the Berlin wall. Even the bizarre joint awarding of the tournament to Japan and South Korea 4 years previously had an apparent motive of reconciliation of two countries who had a long history of enmity, even if everyone knew that co-hosting was the result of irreconcilable differences between the European and Latin American factions within the FIFA executive. England's case was simply 'we can host it and we want to'. The shallowness of England's bid was exemplified by a campaign team that toured the world trying to win votes but only ever speaking in English.

It was reasoned by the FA that it would very much help England's chances if it had more influence in the international corridors of power – in other words, FIFA. That England did not have a representative on the FIFA executive committee was seen as a serious disadvantage. The FA's attempt to gain friends and influence people led to one of the most shameful episodes in the Association's history: the so-called 'cash for votes' scandal of 1998. At UEFA's congress in Dublin in May the FA's Chairman Keith Wiseman and Chief Executive Graham Kelly attempted to have the Scot David Will replaced as the International Football Association Board's representative on the FIFA executive committee. The IFAB was admitted to FIFA in 1928 and was the direct descendant of the FA's International Board, formed in 1886 to standardise the rules of the game. The IFAB is made up of the four representatives from the home nations and four from FIFA. An 80 per cent majority is required for any changes to the rules of the game so Britain has an effective veto over any proposed changes. Unsurprisingly, many view the IFAB as anachronistic and consider its privileged position on the FIFA executive committee unfair. The home associations are fiercely protective of their membership of the IFAB and its existence is the reason why they would never countenance anything – such as an all-British team competing in the World Cup or the Old Firm playing in England – which would undermine their independence.

In order to remove Will from the IFAB the FA needed another two votes and they offered the Welsh FA a £3.2m non-repayable loan in exchange for their support of Wiseman as the Board's representative. The Northern Irish association rejected the FA's approach so, with the Scottish voting for Will, the FA's plan failed. That the plan was ill-conceived is clear: Will was one of just three FIFA executive committee members who voted for England's bid and had Wiseman managed to usurp Will he would not have been able to vote for England's bid, as executive committee members are not allowed to vote for their own associations. England would actually have earned one vote less. Wiseman and Kelly claimed that they were aware of the rule but that the point of the exercise was not to win one vote but to influence a substantial number of the other executive committee members. Instead, all the exercise achieved was to highlight the anomaly of the IFAB's privileged position on FIFA's executive committee, further damage the FA's standing internationally and cost Wiseman and Kelly their jobs. Will went on to remain a highly respected member of FIFA's executive committee and was charged with heading the investigation into its finances. However, that didn't stop Wiseman's successor Geoff Thompson attempting to replace Will with himself once again in 2002. This time all three of the other IFAB members opposed the idea.

That the FA's policy towards FIFA and UEFA was guided simply by its aim to host the 2006 World Cup was exemplified by its decision to support Sepp Blatter rather than UEFA President Lennart Johannsson in the election to the FIFA presidency in 1998. Although Blatter had always expressed a preference for the South African bid, the FA's reasoning was that if South Africa was unable to put together a credible bid, Blatter would switch his support to England rather than Germany. The FA was one of only three of UEFA's 51 federations that voted for Blatter and Johannsson said after his defeat that he felt he had been 'stabbed in the back' by the FA, pointing out that he had supported England's Euro '96 bid and readmission to European club competition after the Heysel ban. So while the FA had gained a friend in Blatter, it had made several other enemies in Europe. In the event South Africa did have a credible bid and the FA had no support from the European members of the executive committee, hence it secured just 3 votes out of a possible 24 in the first-round voting and was eliminated from the second round.

The sacrifice of the FA Cup on the high altar of England's World Cup bid caused irreparable damage to the world's oldest football competition. There is still some dispute as to who asked and who applied pressure on Manchester United to compete in the inaugural World Club Championship in Brazil in 2002, but some facts are clear. The World Club Championship was Sepp Blatter's pet project and fitted in with his plans for FIFA to cash in on the success of club football. The FA and England's World Cup bidding campaign team, with the ministerial support of Tony Banks, were keen for Manchester United to take part but the club, not unreasonably, argued that it already had a crowded fixture list and could not possibly be expected to compete in all domestic and European competitions as well as spend up to a month in Brazil in the middle of the season. Whether the FA or United suggested that the FA Cup not be defended by the holders is unknown but the FA certainly sanctioned their withdrawal. That United's non-participation as holders has undermined the competition is also beyond doubt. How much it contributed to the competition's decline in terms of television viewing figures and attendances is unclear, but it would be naïve to say it had no effect whatsoever. The FA Cup is the FA's primary product in terms of revenue. While the FA makes money from England internationals, the extent of this revenue is contingent on the team's success in the World Cup and the European Championships. The FA Cup television rights are sold as part of a package with England games, currently in a three-year joint deal with Sky and the BBC worth around £400m over three years. It is difficult to analyse viewing figures and attendances for FA Cup rounds on a year-by-year basis because there are very few like-for-like fixtures and even when they do occur, the competing teams will be enjoying different levels of success and support. However, the FA Cup final is a reasonable indicator of public interest and 2002 saw just 6.3 million viewers for Arsenal's defeat of Chelsea, whereas the 1997 final between Chelsea and Middlesbrough was watched by 11.1 million and the figures have declined ever since.

If the cash for votes scandal and the FA's vote for Sepp Blatter in the 1998 FIFA presidential election both damaged the FA's reputation at home and abroad, while the withdrawal of Manchester United from the FA Cup cost the FA dear financially in terms of devaluing the competition, the Wembley saga represents a massive blow to both the FA and England's worldwide reputation. The ever-increasing cost of the project also threatens the finances of the FA itself and its ability to continue its funding of grassroots football, and has placed a strain on its relationship with the government.

The FA bought Wembley for £103m from Wembley plc in March 1998, when the original cost of the project was estimated to be £260m. The National Lottery was to provide £120m and the FA the remainder. The National Lottery funding was under the auspices of the Sports Council, now Sport England, on the understanding that the stadium could be used for athletics and could host the 2005 World Athletics Championships. It is worth noting that the FA had acquired the site at no cost to itself and was already looking at ways that it could build the new stadium without having to spend any of its own money.

The man chosen to lead the project was Chelsea Chairman and FA Director Ken Bates. The choice of Bates was based on his supposed success developing the Stamford Bridge Chelsea Village complex of hotel and leisure businesses, despite the fact that by 1998 that project was behind schedule. Chelsea Village has made a profit in only one of the last five years and last year reported pre-tax losses of £11.1m. Under Bates, plans for Wembley became a 'Chelsea Village Mark Two', writ large, with hotels and office space added to provide additional income streams. However, as the project became more ambitious, so the costs escalated and the latest costing is around £750m. In December 1999 it emerged that the design had quietly dropped the provision for an athletics track, thus removing one of the main reasons why Sport England had provided lottery funding. After three weeks of prevarication, the then Culture Secretary Chris Smith agreed to let the project go ahead without an athletics track if the FA would return £20m of the £120m.

Further costs were added to the project in June 2000 when planning permission was granted by Brent Council but with the proviso that the FA pay for improvements to rail and road links around the site. In July of that year, England lost its bid to host the 2006 World Cup finals, but nobody bothered to draw breath and ask if the now grandiose stadium scheme was justified and it trundled on with costs escalating.

The final match to be played at Wembley was England's one–nil defeat at the hands of Germany in October 2000, Kevin Keegan's last game as manager. With the stadium closed down the American bank Chase Manhattan did the rounds of the City banks in an attempt to raise the £410m that was now needed to fund the project. Chase's role was to present a business plan that would show the project was financially viable. The project still bore the Ken Bates trademark, with offices and hotels incorporated into the scheme, designed to yield revenues that would then be used to pay back the loan. The problem with the business plan was that it implicitly admitted that the stadium alone was not financially viable and that it needed other ancillary businesses to be profitable in order for the loan to be repaid.

Bates was replaced as Chairman of Wembley National Stadium Limited by Sir Rodney Walker and resigned from the board in February 2001. In May, the FA Chief Executive released a statement asking the Government to bail the project out. The statement reveals the FA's thinking about its place in the scheme:

> When we first took on the development through our subsidiary, WNSL, it was agreed by all parties that the FA should be ring-

fenced from any potential financial liabilities. In other words, the FA – other than staging events at the stadium – would not contribute any money whatsoever.

The financial model on which the project was based, supported by specialist advice, has proved over time to be flawed and the banks now require full financial recourse to the FA. Effectively, we are being asked to save this project rather than just give a commitment to stage our events at the stadium.

The sums of money involved are staggering. Under the current proposals, the FA would have to pay £125m in equity plus £55m per annum for the debt-term, as well as funding any construction over-runs which are common in a project of this kind.

The FA simply cannot afford, as a not-for-profit organisation, to act as the sole sponsor of the scheme – the scale of the commitment required would put our own future in jeopardy and the development of football throughout the country.[1]

Crozier admitted then that the FA never intended to pay a penny for the stadium, which was to be its headquarters and form the centrepiece of its 2006 World Cup bid. It wanted to have control of the stadium's use and how it was financed, but it was not prepared to even guarantee the debts incurred. The admission that the financial model was 'flawed' meant that Bates' position was untenable and he obviously had to go in order for the scheme to salvage any credibility. The difference between Bates' view of the Government's role in the scheme and that of Crozier was illustrated by Bates' evidence to the House Of Commons Culture Media and Sport Committee in March, just weeks before Crozier appealed to the Government to bail out the project. Bates told the committee: 'My personal feeling is . . . the fact of the matter is that the Government have no legal standing in this matter. They have no finance in it; they have assumed an importance beyond their station.' Bates claimed that the £120m of lottery money 'is not public money. It came from the lottery money provided by the ordinary people of this country'. When Bates resigned from the WNSL board he launched a stinging attack on both the FA and former Sports Minister Kate Hoey, much of which he repeated in his evidence to the Commons select committee. Bates described the management of WNSL by the FA as 'a committee being run by a committee' and with characteristic modesty likened his role to that of Jesus Christ, claiming: 'Even Jesus Christ suffered only one Pontius Pilate – I had a whole team of them.'

It is true that the FA is a not-for-profit organisation, but it certainly doesn't behave like one, not least in paying its chief executive a £418,000 salary. Out of a turnover of £109m in 2000, the FA's costs were around £40m, of which staff costs were £16m. Indeed, the FA doesn't make a profit, but then doesn't try to. Of the £109m of income it received, around £100m came from the BBC/Sky deal. If it is going to be able to fund the development of the grass-roots game at the level that it has previously it will be hoping that its next TV deal is worth at least as much as before, otherwise it will have to make cuts. Ominously, Sky has recently said that it may not bid for the FA Cup rights next time they become available in 2004.

The Government turned down Crozier's plea for a bailout and instead Tony Blair ordered an inquiry into the whole project, including whether Wembley was indeed the right venue for a national stadium. The results of the inquiry were never made public but the Government eventually gave the go-ahead for the project. The Government select committee met again in May 2002 and heard evidence from management consultants Tropus, who were involved in the early stages of the project and who were highly critical of the way that the decision was made to award the contract to rebuild Wembley to the Australian construction company Multiplex. Tropus chairman David Hudson told the committee: 'It became increasingly clear from early in 1999 that the project was not being managed in a way that we would have expected in that the processes and procedures did not follow those that we would expect to see on any significant project and particularly a major project such as this.' Specifically, Hudson claimed that Multiplex was given information that helped it formulate its bid that was not made available to other potential bidders for the work. 'The competition that was put in place was clearly not fair in our opinion,' he said. 'More directly damaging to the project, in our professional view, were the irregularities in the construction procurement and decisions made in regard thereto.' Multiplex had guaranteed to complete the project for a fixed price of £326m but that price was said only to be guaranteed until the beginning of May 2002. Multiplex were also awarded the contract to build the new West Stand at Stamford Bridge, for an undisclosed sum.

In the nick of time, the FA finally managed to find someone to lend it the £400m now required to complete the project in the form of the German bank West LB. There was still a shortfall of around £200m but the FA, the Greater London Assembly and Sport England are supposed to find that. Although 'heads of agreement' have been signed between the FA and West LB and the Government has given the project the go-ahead again, it would surely be a brave person who would bet against seeing the ubiquitous headline 'Wembley Project Delayed' again.

The FA's handling of the Wembley fiasco may just seem to be an example of incompetence, but the influence of the doomed 2006 World Cup bid is all over the project. It was not just the original reason for the new Wembley, it contributed to the way the project was run from day one. Former Sports Minister Kate Hoey claimed that any criticism of the way the Wembley project was being handled was deemed to be sabotaging the bid itself and consequently any dissent was decidedly muted. In May 2002 the former Chief Executive of WNSL Bob Stubbs delivered his verdict on the FA's handling of the project: 'I don't think the FA is competent to deliver. The individuals are competent but the culture and structure of the organisation will not facilitate delivery of the project.' The World Cup bid became an unstoppable train for the FA, once it was decided to bid, everything was sublimated to this process. The FA's relationship with UEFA, the credibility of the FA Cup and the future of Wembley Stadium were all gambled on winning the right to host the 2006 World Cup finals. A gamble that failed miserably. What is amazing about the Wembley fiasco, however, was that it continued even after the bid had failed. After the cash for votes scandal and Manchester United's withdrawal from the FA Cup, the FA made strenuous efforts to re-brand and restructure itself and rebuild its reputation both domestically and internationally. Unfortunately, the Wembley fiasco undermined those efforts.

Following the resignation of Kelly and the sacking of Wiseman (Kelly left with dignity but Wiseman refused to budge, claiming he had done nothing wrong, and had to be sacked), the FA decided to seize the day and re-brand itself while appointing a new chief executive and chairman. The FA council remained the ultimate authority but a new 13-man board was given executive powers to run the game. The balance of power still resided with the amateur game with six members representing county associations and five from the professional game. The Premier League has four representatives on the board – at the time of writing they were Leeds United Chief Executive Peter Ridsdale, Premier League Chairman David Richards, Arsenal Chief Executive David Dein and Chelsea Chairman Ken Bates. The Football League is represented by Peter Heard, Chairman of Colchester United. The other two members of the FA board are FA Chairman Geoff Thompson and Chief Executive Adam Crozier. Crozier, a former advertising executive and, more controversially, a Scot, was brought in as the new broom to change the culture of the FA. The phrase 'replacing blazers with suits' seemed apposite at the time but Crozier didn't even wear a tie! The Association embarked on a graduate-recruitment programme in order to inject some new blood into the bureaucracy, seen to be stifling the organisation, and adding a sense of dynamism. Lancaster Gate was sold and offices in Soho Square were rented while the FA waited for the new Wembley to be built, where it planned to locate its new headquarters. The third-round draw for the 2000 FA Cup was a shining example of the FA's 'newness'. The FA's Executive Director David Davies, a new post, introduced the televised draw from the new headquarters of the FA in Soho Square. Not only was there a new format with an invited audience, but there were even new balls in a new bag. There was also the uniquely new concept of the 'lucky loser', who had lost in the second round but was drawn out of a hat to join the third round in place of the withdrawn Manchester United. There was more than a little consternation that while Darlington had lost to Gillingham, who were rewarded with a home tie against Walsall, the lucky losers drew a lucrative fixture away at Aston Villa.

Despite the FA's efforts to modernise, it remains essentially a nineteenth-century organisation struggling to adapt to the twenty-first-century market economy. The balance of power on the board is still in favour of the amateur game but the make-up of the FA council, to which the board is ultimately answerable, is even more biased to the amateur game with the vast majority of the 92 councillors drawn from the county associations with the interests of the universities, schools and the armed forces represented by councillors. The professional game is represented at committee level but the power of these committees has come under question. For example, Bates is a member of the Challenge Cup committee that oversees the FA Cup. However, the controversial decision to play the 2002 FA Cup semi-final between Fulham and Chelsea at Villa Park instead of in London was made without reference to that committee, as was the decision to play the match on a Sunday evening, which resulted in many supporters arriving home in the early hours of Monday morning. The FA's commercial department, which is answerable to the chairman and chief executive, decided to hold the tie around 100 miles from London in order to maximise ticket sales and corporate-hospitality revenue. Bates said of the decision:

> There were 6,000 seats unsold at Villa Park and overall I reckon fans spent between £2m and £3m in travel to the two semis with the cost of coaches and fuel. The decisions about the venues were taken by the FA. In future they should be made by the Challenge Cup committee who are football people. The committee was not consulted on prices, location or kick-off times. They were all decided by the FA's commercial department.

Bates' comments highlight the problematic relationship between the professional game and the FA. The FA no longer acts as a brake on professionalism, but rather as a competing commercial entity. Nothing exemplifies this relationship more than the continuing club v. country debate. Clubs pay the wages of players who then compete and earn money for the national team, sometimes picking up injuries that keep them from playing for their clubs on their return. Naturally clubs resent this state of affairs and the G14 group has been campaigning that national federations should at least pay an insurance premium so that clubs can be compensated should their players be injured while on international duty. The club v. country debate is not confined to England and with so many foreign players in the English game, even tournaments such as the African Cup of Nations can denude squads for long periods of time. True, clubs are aware when they sign players that they may be required for international duty, but the demands of the international fixture list are becoming more onerous. FIFA's new international co-ordinated calendar is an attempt to overcome the club v. country dilemma, but as yet it is not possible to see how effective it will be in doing so.

In the now infamous *Blueprint for the Future of Football* that the FA produced in 1992 to justify its backing of the breakaway Premier League, it was claimed that the FA was planning to remodel itself on Germany's

Deutscher Fussball Bund. The DFB had total control of professional football in Germany, running the professional league, selling its TV rights and redistributing the income throughout the game. It also policed the finances of the clubs through a strict licensing scheme that prohibits clubs from running up debts. The FA deduced that the success of the German national team – it had won the 1990 World Cup – was due to the regulatory structure of the German game and thought that if it could replicate the German system then success for the England team would follow. The problem with this reasoning was that German clubs were run on a not-for-profit basis and the divide between the professional and the amateur clubs was not as marked as it was in England. Nor was there a rival body, like the Football League, to challenge the authority of the DFB and it was able to run the game unopposed. In order for the FA to become an English DFB it would have to take over the clubs and then licence them back to their owners – hardly what the First Division chairmen had in mind when they sought the FA's support for a breakaway.

The FA has failed to establish anything like the control over the Premier League that the DFB has over the German professional game and, given the historical differences in football in both countries, that is hardly surprising. The FA has a financial-compliance unit, manned by two people, but it does not monitor clubs' liquidity in the way that the DFB does. If it did, perhaps the English game would not be cursed with at least £700m of debt. The main benefit of the German model, however, is that it allows all football TV rights to be sold in a co-ordinated manner, with packages made available for competing broadcasters. The DFB sells the rights for the national team, the Bundesliga and the German Cup, and can sell mixed packages. At present the FA sells the FA Cup and England home games as a package, but cannot sell Premier League rights. This means that it is in direct competition with the Premier League, rather than working in co-operation with it. It is worth noting, however, that the German system has come under review recently and the Bundesliga is moving towards a limited amount of independence from the DFB. German clubs have complained that the strict financial controls have limited their ability to raise capital and compete with clubs from the rest of Europe, and there have been changes in the law that have enabled clubs such as Borussia Dortmund to float on the German stock market. That said, even when the reforms are completed, it is unlikely that the DFB will have ceded control of the

German game to the clubs to the extent that the FA has.

That the FA has abrogated its role as the ultimate authority in the English game is exemplified by its response to the current crisis. As shown in Chapter 1, it has tried to distance itself from the Wimbledon decision, somehow contriving to express regret that the club is relocating, while doing absolutely nothing to stop it. The FA has expressed no concern about the level of debt that the game has accrued and its financial-compliance unit has only seen fit to investigate the finances of two clubs, Chesterfield and Boston United. It has done little to curb the influence of players' agents or police the transfer market and turned a blind eye to the flouting of its Rule 34 limiting dividend payments and the winding up of clubs, before quietly dropping the rule. Its plan to restore its position at the top of the English game, attempting to see off the challenge of the Football League by backing the breakaway Premier League, has merely created a new, and stronger, third force in the sport.

With a turnover of over £100m a year the Football Association earns less than Manchester United but more than any other English club. Its income is mainly derived from the sale of TV and sponsorship rights to the FA Cup and the England team, with a significant contribution from corporate hospitality and ticket sales for the FA Cup final and semi-finals and home England games. In that way it is similar to a club, but the big difference is that it does not pay players' wages. It pays players while they are on England duty but it has no other obligations to them. What the FA does not pay players it spends on developing the game and distributes it to the grass-roots, which includes 40,000 clubs playing in 2,200 leagues. Over the next three years the FA has committed over £50m to the grass-roots and £11m for the women's game. Capital projects include the building of the National Football Centre near Burton-upon-Trent at an estimated cost of £50m. The commitment to these projects is laudable and does give the FA a certain purpose, but their costs mean that it is essential that there are no liabilities arising from the Wembley fiasco. This is what Crozier meant when he said: 'The FA simply cannot afford, as a not-for-profit organisation, to act as the sole sponsor of the scheme – the scale of the commitment required would put our own future in jeopardy and the development of football throughout the country.' What he forgot to add is that the FA cannot afford for the project to be cancelled either. Having spent over £100m of somebody else's money acquiring Wembley, the FA would have to repay £120m that it simply does not have. The land value of the Wembley site is £64.5m so even if it sold the site, the FA would have to find over £55m. This is why the FA still remains committed to Wembley as the site of the national stadium – even though there are cheaper alternatives, including a site in the Midlands or the option of not having a national stadium at all but playing England games at club grounds, which is popular with supporters, and FA Cup finals at the Millennium Stadium in Cardiff.

Wembley is the FA's legacy from its failed 2006 World Cup bid. One ill-conceived project begat another, but after the bid failed, it was too late to drop the Wembley development. The FA has done nothing to suggest that it ever had the expertise to oversee the project but convinced itself that the likes of Ken Bates could deliver. At a meeting of the FA council in September 1999, around the time when the running track was dropped, Wembley was on the agenda but the only question asked was by Noel White about the positioning of the coaches' benches. The FA Council, which is mainly representative of the amateur game, is hardly equipped to monitor the progress of the project, nor would seem to have the will. The best way forward for Wembley would be for the government to take it over, underwrite the financing and then lease it back to the FA on an annual basis. That way the FA could still make some money out of the new stadium, which has been its overriding concern from day one, but would not have its future put in doubt. More importantly, the new stadium may actually be built, on schedule and at a predetermined cost. Perhaps without the distraction of Wembley, the FA could focus on trying to lead football out of its current crisis.

## ENDNOTE

[1] WNSL Statement, 1 May 2002 (online press release)

# 9. Players, Agents and the Union

WHILE THE FOOTBALL ASSOCIATION, THE FOOTBALL LEAGUE AND THE PREMIER LEAGUE ARE engaged in a power struggle for control of the game, the single most powerful interest group consists of the players themselves. This should come as no surprise as it was football players, albeit gentlemen amateurs, that founded the game and set up the Football Association. Football in England became established because people wanted to play it; the structures within which it was played arose because people wanted to watch other people play the game and were prepared to pay to do so.

The modern professional footballer has a unique position in society. On the one hand some are treated like film stars and can command massive salaries. Yet, as David Beckham was negotiating a new £100,000-a-week contract, there were newspaper stories claiming as many as 800 players could be without a club at the start of the following season. Although some players earn fortunes and enjoy millionaire lifestyles, they display many of the characteristics of the old working class. Practically nobody else in modern Britain has remuneration described in weekly terms anymore, yet players' wages are always expressed as a weekly wage. The FA's Chief Executive Adam Crozier, for example, is never referred to as the £8,000-a-week Scot. There is another aspect of the modern footballer that seems like a throwback to a class-divided industrial society: a closed-shop trade union with a propensity to threaten industrial action. The PFA appears to be one of the strongest unions in Britain with a membership that is incredibly loyal to its leadership. The union has become a fourth force in the governance of the English game, and a force to be reckoned with as the Premier League, Football Association and the Football League found when they attempted to take on the union over its share of TV money in 2001.

Although modern footballers have many of the characteristics of the proletarian labourer, they also employ agents like actors or models, or even writers. The agents themselves have become immensely powerful within the game and have now formed companies that are quoted on the stock exchange. England has more registered player agents than any other country, which is hardly surprising as England has more professional players than any other country, with 100 clubs employing 4,000 full-time players. There is the added complication that the PFA also doubles as an agent for some players.

As the FA forbade professionalism until 1885, the first professional players were paid clandestinely, and it is impossible to ascertain who the first professional footballers were. However, Russell in *Football and the English* cites the case of J.J. Lang who played for Sheffield Wednesday in the 1876–77 season and was given a job in a local knife-making works after arriving from Scotland. In fact early professionalism was characterised by illicit payments and sinecures. Amateur clubs were allowed to pay expenses for broken time and travelling but very often these were inflated, and much of the FA's time in the 1870s and '80s was spent adjudicating on disputes over payments to players, as detailed in Chapter 2.[1]

When professionalism was legalised in 1885 it might have been expected to lead to an increase in the rights of players and generally improve their lot. However, this was not to be the case as the clubs imposed the retain and transfer system that was to characterise players' status for a hundred years until the Bosman ruling of 1995. Prior to 1885, players were free to change clubs at will and frequently did so. With the advent of professionalism, clubs sought to protect their investment and did so with the help of the FA which took control of players' registrations. The retain and transfer system firmly established the relationship between the upper, middle and entrepreneurial classes that owned the clubs and ran the game through the FA, and the working-class players. At first the FA was keen to outlaw transfer fees but faced opposition from the Football League and eventually settled on a role policing transfers with an array of sanctions at its disposal. The first £1,000 transfer in 1905 of Alf Common from Sunderland to Middlesbrough saw the FA try and impose a maximum transfer fee of £350, but clubs soon found ways of circumventing the maximum and it was dropped.

The FA and the League were agreed on one issue, however: the maximum wage, which was introduced in 1900 at the level of £4 per week. The clubs and the FA both had an interest in keeping wage levels to a minimum, but for the clubs this was tempered by the desire to employ the best players. So collectively the clubs were in favour of the maximum wage, while individually they would seek to circumvent it. This gave the FA a new role; whereas in the 1880s it constantly disciplined clubs for making payments to players, which were outlawed with the ban on professionalism, from 1900 to 1961, when the maximum wage was abolished, it was concerned with policing the maximum wage. This kept the FA busy as there were many cases of clubs being disciplined for making illegal payments. Manchester City were found to be paying players £6 10s a week plus bonuses in 1905; 17 players were suspended by the League and all the directors were forced to resign.

Given the fact that the legalisation of professionalism cast players firmly in the role of workers, it is hardly surprising that the players formed their own union in 1907. Russell points to the fact that trade unionism was on the increase in the 1900s and the 1906 Trade Disputes Act gave unions more rights. Russell also suggests that the music-hall performers' strike of 1906 may have been an inspiration. The Association Football Players Union was originally formed by two Manchester United players Billy Meredith and Charlie Roberts and had its first dispute with the FA in 1909. The union wanted to affiliate to the National Federation of Trade Unions, an early version of the TUC, and the FA threatened to withdraw recognition of the players' union. The union, for its part, threatened to strike. The start of the season was put back by a week as the dispute dragged on and eventually a compromise was reached. The union agreed that players would work under the jurisdiction of the FA if the FA would recognise the union and allow the union recourse to law. The FA agreed but insisted that the union disaffiliate from the NFTU. The issue went to a ballot of the players, who voted against strike action.

The union first challenged the retain and transfer system in 1912 when it took Aston Villa to court, but lost and saw its membership decline up to the outbreak of the First World War. In 1923, with trade unionism on the rise nationally, the union took Chesterfield to court in a test case when the Football League tried to impose a wage cut on players who were under contract. The union won the case on appeal and from then on its membership and influence increased. While the formation of the union was in response to the FA and the League's treatment of players as labourers, it succeeded in uniting both against the union. The FA and the Football League may have been engaged in a power struggle from the 1880s to the present, but they have been united against the players' union.

That the maximum wage survived until 1961 was partly due to the fact that it was deemed an essential part of the sport by the governing body, and partly due to the Professional Footballers Association (PFA) (as the union was known after its name change in 1958) accepting it, preferring instead to concentrate on welfare issues. All that was to change in the late 1950s. The advent of televised football and a deal with the pools companies meant that there was more money in the game. At the same time there was a general increase in wages nationally in the era when Macmillan told the British people 'You've never had it so good'. The PFA not only wanted an end to the maximum wage but also to the retain and transfer system. By combining their demands, the PFA ensured that they would get a hostile response from the Football League, which at a 1960 extraordinary general meeting offered only to consider raising the maximum wage.

In his seminal history of the Football League, *The Football League and the Men Who Made It*, Simon Inglis identifies three factors that strengthened the PFA's case. The transfer of John Charles from Leeds to Juventus in 1957 showed that the English game was behind the continent financially. With Brian Clough and Jimmy Greaves reportedly targets for Italian clubs, the PFA argued that many English players would leave the country to seek better remuneration abroad. A case involving five Sunderland players who were fined and suspended by the FA and the League had gone to court and the players had won. The PFA believed that it had a legal case and that if the dispute over the maximum wage and the retain and transfer system went to court it would win that case too. Thirdly, the PFA Chief Executive Jimmy Hill had lobbied the media relentlessly and had a high profile that was at variance with the image of the bureaucrats at the FA and the League. Hill believed, rightly as it turned out, that the public would support the players. It is worth noting at this point that in all subsequent disputes between the PFA and the football authorities, the PFA usually won the PR battle. The reasons for this will be discussed further when looking at the TV money dispute of 2001, but League Secretary Alan Hardaker acknowledged the point: 'The clubs were wrong in their attitude, they were wrong in the way they handled their case, and public opinion was against them.'² Essentially the difference between the rival campaigns was that Hill portrayed it as a matter of principle while the League saw it as just a matter of money and thought that by offering more money they could avoid changes to the fundamental relationship between players and their clubs.

In the late 1950s and early 1960s industrial disputes were often arbitrated by the government's Ministry of Labour, and the PFA's dispute with the League was such a case. In December 1960 the Ministry put forward a compromise position that allowed the maximum wage to be raised to £30 a week for two years, after which it would be abolished. The retain and transfer system would be reformed to allow three-year contracts, all previous contracts were for one year, and a panel would be set up to arbitrate on contract disputes between clubs and players. The League chairmen rejected the proposals and a players' strike was called for on Saturday, 21 January 1961. What became clear in the run-up to the strike was that the clubs would rather give ground on the maximum wage than on the retain and transfer system. Some wealthy clubs had wanted an end to the maximum wage for some time. Fulham, for example, had said that Johnny Haynes was worth £100 a week and Tottenham had wanted to increase players' wages since 1950. Three days before the strike was due to take place an agreement was reached at the offices of the Ministry of Labour whereby the maximum wage was abolished with immediate effect and changes were made to the retain and transfer system. The changes were superficial rather than fundamental; players could not be transferred while under contract without the players' consent and a League committee was to arbitrate if the player and the club could not agree on terms or a transfer. Within weeks of the dispute being settled Fulham agreed to pay Johnny Haynes £100 per week, five times the previous maximum.

It is impossible to underestimate the effect of the abolition of the maximum wage on English football. From 18 January 1961, most of the money that has come into English football has gone to the players. That is not to suggest that there is anything wrong with that, after all the fundamental premise of professional football is people paying to watch other people playing the game. The clubs act as conduits for that money and if the money has to go anywhere then the players are surely the most worthy recipients of it. In the 1960s clubs used all their income either to buy players or pay their wages, as is the case today. But the abolition of the maximum wage facilitated inflationary drivers into the game that had previously been held in check. When there was a maximum on the amount clubs could pay players, the ways that rich clubs could utilise their economic superiority over other clubs were limited to illicit bonus payments, the standard of competition they could provide and the opportunity to win honours. After 1961, rich clubs could simply outbid poorer clubs for the best players and players could ask for as much as a club could afford and be confident of getting it. Player wage inflation was born in 1961 and the game is still struggling to come to terms with it.

If the League thought they had seen off any challenges to the retain and transfer system they were mistaken. George Eastham had failed to persuade Newcastle to let him transfer to Arsenal in 1960 and called on the union for help. Although he eventually made the move, the PFA used his as a test case in the courts and in 1963 Mr Justice Wilberforce ruled that the retain and transfer system was 'an unjustifiable restraint of trade'. What the ruling meant was that a club had the right to retain a player as long as it could match the terms being offered by another club. If a club did not want to retain a player it could let him go on a free transfer or sell him for an agreed fee. Although this was a victory for players and a vast improvement on the system that pertained prior to 1963, their careers were still determined by the clubs. If a club wanted to retain a player it only had to match any offers in terms of wages and could always place an artificially high price on a player's head.

The events of 1961 and 1963 radically transformed the relationship between the players and their clubs and consequently the economics of football. For 80 years football had operated in isolation from the rest of the economy. Club income was determined by how many people turned up to watch matches, but outgoings were strictly controlled thanks to the maximum wage. Players could be retained or sold with no concern as to their own wishes and without a signing-on fee, with all the proceeds going to the selling club. It is fair to say that the modern game, and the current crisis it is in, was born in the early 1960s. Top players went from being wage labourers to stars in the space of three years, and stars need agents, or so agents would have them believe.

Players' agents have been involved in the game at least since the legalisation of professionalism in 1886. Early agents worked principally for clubs, acting as scouts to unearth new talent. From the early 1950s a new breed of agent started to emerge who represented players' interests. Because of the maximum wage restriction their first area of business was in arranging product endorsements for their clients, such as Everton's Dixie Dean who was said to have earned £50 a year for endorsing a number of products. Even in the early days of player agency, agents were unpopular with clubs and during the 1960 maximum wage dispute League Secretary Alan Hardaker claimed the whole dispute had been engineered by an agent called Bagenal Harvey. Harvey, an early version of the modern agent, built his career representing the cricketer Dennis Compton, arranging his lucrative endorsement of Brylcreem. The end of the maximum wage and the reform of the retain and transfer system in the early 1960s increased the earning power of players and allowed them to change clubs and renegotiate their contracts more freely. Research by Szymanski and Kuypers in *Winners and Losers: The Business Strategy of Football* reveals that between 1960 and 1964 First Division wages increased by 61 per cent, and for all players by 54 per cent. Agents then became involved in negotiating with clubs on behalf of players and as the value of contracts increased so agencies became more lucrative.

In 1978 the concept of free agency was established after the government's Commission on Industrial Relations instigated talks between the Football League and the PFA. The League agreed that when a player reached the end of his contract the club could choose to offer a contract on at least as good terms as the previous one, release the player on a free transfer or sell him for a transfer fee. In any circumstances, when a player reached the end of his contract he was free to move to another club of his choice if it was prepared to offer him acceptable terms. In exchange for these major concessions, the PFA lifted their ban on foreign players and a tribunal was set up to arbitrate on disputes over transfer fees.

The immediate effect of the 1978 freedom of contract was a massive increase in transfer fees. Prior to 1978 the highest transfer fee received by an English club was the £500,000 that Hamburg paid Liverpool for Kevin Keegan, while the highest fee paid was £325,000 by Liverpool to Middlesbrough for Graeme Souness. In 1979 the £1m barrier was smashed when Birmingham sold Trevor Francis to Nottingham Forest for £1.18m. There was also another increase in wages; Szymanski and Kuypers calculate that First Division wages increased by an average 24 per cent a year for the four years following freedom of contract. Perhaps more significantly, the percentage of football clubs' income that was spent on wages was 51 per cent in the ten years following freedom of contract, compared to 46 per cent in the ten years previous.

The 1995 Bosman ruling completed the transition of footballers from wage labourers to sports stars. Out-of-contract Belgian player Jean-Marc Bosman wanted to move from RC Liege to the French club Dunkerque but the Belgian club demanded a transfer fee that was beyond the means of Dunkerque. Bosman took his case to the European Court which ruled that the transfer system contravened Article 48 of the Treaty of Rome by restricting the free movement of labour between EU member states. Although the ruling concerned the movement of players between countries that were members of the European Union, the implication was that transfer fees for out-of-contract players were illegal. The Football Association responded by changing the English rules so that no fee could be demanded for an out-of-contract player over the age of 21.

Just as all previous reforms of the retain and transfer system led to an increase in player wages, so did the Bosman ruling. Apart from the timing of the Bosman ruling, occurring when English football was entering the boom phase which would have led to an increase in wages anyway, the fact that players could be secured on free transfers led clubs to use the money that would previously have been paid to other clubs in transfer fees to attract out-of-contract players. Rather than pay a club £5m for a player and £5m in wages over five years, for example, a club could pay a free agent £7m over five years and make a saving. Of course, such is the nature of the economics of football, clubs didn't actually save any money and spent all the money – and some more – they would have paid in transfer fees in wages.

The effect of the Bosman ruling on player wages was not immediate as many players were still under contract in 1995. However, in the five years from the 1993–94 season to the 1998–99 season Premier League wages rose by an astonishing 266 per cent. In the Football League growth was less dramatic, but still marked, with wages rising by 117.3 per cent. What is alarming is that the increase in wages was not matched by a concomitant increase in income. Premier League income rose by 177 per cent and Football League income by 108 per cent.

Another effect of the Bosman ruling was a tendency for contracts to be written for a longer period. With players able to move for no fee at the end of their contracts, the only way that a club could recoup its investment in players was to sell them while they were still under contract. Therefore the longer the contract, the greater the chance of receiving a fee. Another reason for longer contracts was that players would negotiate a new contract as their old one drew to a close. If a club wanted to retain a player whose contract was due to expire, the club would need to offer a new contract with improved terms before the current contract expired. The longer the contract the fewer opportunities for renegotiation occurred. The tendency for longer contracts is one of the major contributors to football's current crisis. Because of concern from both the English and European competition authorities, television deals are becoming shorter, most of the major English TV deals are now for three years, while player contracts are becoming longer. When player contracts are longer than television contracts, there is no guarantee that the funds will be available to honour the player contract once the television deal has expired. Football League clubs are struggling to meet their commitments to players after the collapse of the ITV Digital deal, but Premier League clubs could find themselves in the same position if the next television deal is worth less than the current one and they have players still under contracts signed when the expectation was that it would be worth more.

The modern football agent has prospered since the Bosman ruling. Transfers still take place and have increased in value. The increase in player wages has meant an increase in agents' fees and the practice of renegotiating contracts mid-term has meant that they can also earn commission without a player moving clubs and when they are still under contract. There are 179 FIFA-registered agents in England, compared to 88 in France, 80 in Germany, 56 in Spain and 54 in Italy. In order to become a FIFA-registered agent a bond of 100,000 Swiss francs (around £43,000) is required. The only people exempt from paying the bond are relatives of players and qualified lawyers and accountants. There are no other qualifications needed to become an agent and they are drawn from a variety of backgrounds. Some are ex-players like Cyril Regis and Jesper Olson, others like Eric Hall and Athol Still have moved into football after representing performing artists. One of the most successful players' agents is Jon Holmes, who used to be a life-insurance salesman.

The world of players' agents is a secretive one; few details ever emerge about the level of commission that they receive on deals or who they actually represent. The agents themselves do not have to disclose how much they earn from deals, and clubs, despite often bemoaning agents in general, rarely divulge details of their dealings with them. Only when a complaint is made do any details emerge about their *modus operandi* and the levels of commission they can command.

When Duncan Ferguson returned to Everton in 2000, the move nearly fell through because Ferguson claimed that Newcastle owed £1m in compensation for selling him while he was still under contract. It later emerged that it was not Ferguson who was holding out for the compensation, but his agent Dennis Roach, who Bobby Robson branded a 'parasite'. Roach, also former England Manager Glenn Hoddle's agent, was later charged by the FA with misconduct over his handling of the transfer and that of Paulo Wanchope from West Ham to Manchester City. The FA charged Roach with contravention of four of their regulations, which state:

- an agent shall act at all times in an ethical and professional manner and shall observe the highest standards of integrity and fair dealing;
- an agent shall act for only one party in a transaction;
- an agent shall be entitled to payment in relation to a relevant transaction from his principal only and shall not accept any other payment in relation to such transaction;
- an agent shall take all possible steps to promote the reputation of the game of association football and to prevent it being brought into disrepute.[3]

Roach, who former Derby Manager Jim Smith once accused of sabotaging the transfer of Jonatan Johansson from Rangers to the Midlands club because he demanded £250,000 'just for sending a fax', took the FA to the High Court in November 2001, arguing that as he was licensed by FIFA, only FIFA had the authority to discipline him.[4] The case was then referred to FIFA in January 2002 and has yet to be heard.

The saga of Nicolas Anelka's protracted transfer from Arsenal to Real Madrid illustrates both the flaws in the transfer regulations and the role of the modern agent. The player was under contract at Arsenal but made no secret of his desire to leave the club. He originally approached Marseille in early May 1999 to try and negotiate a move back to France, but soon his brother – and agent – Claude was in talks with Real Madrid. Arsenal complained to FIFA that Madrid had made an illegal approach: 'The player has a four-year contract, and any direct approach to the player is illegal,' said Arsenal Manager Arsène Wenger.[5] Lazio soon entered into direct negotiations with Arsenal, but Anelka's brother was insistent that the Spanish club would get their man, even though there had been no direct approach by Madrid. Eventually Lazio grew frustrated and withdrew their offer in late July. Madrid finally approached Arsenal and agreed a £23.5m fee for the player who signed a seven-year deal on 1 August.

Arsenal Chief Executive David Dein was scathing: 'In the space of 48 hours Anelka and Jimmy Floyd Hasselbaink have ridden roughshod over all the rules of English football and shown a huge lack of respect for the fans and what the game should stand for.'[6]

Dein's main concern was the way that players and their agents can effectively tear up their contracts and choose to play for whoever they want, irrespective of whether they are under contract or not. Another issue raised was the role of agents and how they can tout a player around clubs while he is under contract. There was also the issue of clubs approaching players directly without the permission of the players' clubs. The Anelka and Hasselbaink cases (Hasselbaink adopted similar tactics to Anelka in order to secure a transfer from Leeds United to Atletico Madrid), show that, for all the supposed regulation of the transfer system, if players or their agents want to instigate a move they can. There is a feeling in football boardrooms that the pendulum of power has swung too far in the direction of players, after being given a push by agents.

There is also growing concern about the possible conflicts of interest involving agents, particularly where club managers have relatives who are also agents. Manchester United's Sir Alex Ferguson, Crystal Palace's Trevor Francis, Bolton's Sam Allardyce and Portsmouth's Harry Redknapp all have sons who are agents, as does Nottingham Forest's Manager Paul Hart whose son Jamie Hart works for the Proactive Sports agency. *The Observer* newspaper revealed on 19 May 2002 that Hart junior handled Jermaine Jenas, who was transferred from Forest to Newcastle in February 2000 for £5m. The paper also revealed that Newcastle Manager Bobby Robson was a shareholder in Proactive as was the club's Chairman Freddy Shepherd. Proactive's Chief Executive Paul Stretford answered allegations of nepotism by saying 'nepotism is not a crime', adding: 'There's a potential conflict of interest on lots of occasions but it depends on how that is managed and conducted. And so long as it's conducted professionally then I really don't see what the problem is.'

*The Observer* also revealed that several managers were shareholders in Proactive. Manchester City's Kevin Keegan, Sunderland's Peter Reid, Blackburn Rovers' Graeme Souness in addition to Newcastle's Robson have all bought players represented by Proactive for their clubs while they were shareholders of Proactive. None of the managers could have been said to have gained personally from the deals, however, as Proactive shares, in common with those of quoted football clubs and the shares of practically every other publicly quoted company, have dived with the rest of the stock market.

The idea of floating player agencies on the stock market appeared to be a good one at the time. After the disappointing performance of shares that followed the dash to the stock market for football clubs in 1996–97 it became apparent that all the money that was going into the game was going straight out of it and into players' and agents' bank accounts. The changes to the transfer system that followed the Bosman ruling meant that players and agents looked set to be the winners. With the flotation of player agencies it appeared as if investors at last had a way of passively making money out of football. Agents Barry Gold and Bill Jennings took Premier Management to the stock market in July 2001 and the shares have since fallen from a launch price of 28p to 20p by July 2002. The same month Stretford's Proactive joined the market and suffered a similar fate, falling from a launch price of 28.5p to 7p a year later. Jon Smith's First Artists joined the stock market from the junior Ofex market in December 2001 and saw its shares fall from 52p to 40p by July 2002. While it is true that nearly all shares have fallen since September 2001, the quoted player agencies have fallen by more than the FTSE all-share index.

The Chairman of Proactive is former Sheffield United Chief Executive Charles Green, who explained to the trade magazine *Football Business International* in August 2001 how Proactive was planning to deliver value for shareholders. He said that with 200 players on its books the company expected to negotiate 100 transfer or contract deals a year. That means that each player will be expected to move or negotiate a new deal with his existing club every two years. Given that contracts are getting longer and four-year deals are becoming the norm, it is clear that in order for Proactive and its shareholders to prosper, there will have to be a lot of players expressing a desire to move while under contract. Green spoke the truth about player agency that most agents usually keep to themselves – the way to make money is to unsettle players and have them change clubs as frequently as possible. The one-club player who spends his career at the same club and is willing to accept what the club thinks he is worth is of no value whatsoever to today's corporate agencies.

If there is a potential conflict of interests between the listed agencies and their shareholders who are managers, a potentially greater one exists for the PFA. The PFA acts as an agent for a number of players, yet it also receives the contract details of every player in English football. When a PFA representative enters the boardroom to negotiate a deal on behalf of a member it is forearmed with the knowledge of the details of every other player at the club. Many other agents resent this advantage that the PFA has over them and want the PFA to cease its agency role, but that looks unlikely as it makes the PFA a substantial amount of money, and after the union's victory over the Premier League, Football League and FA in the autumn of 2001 few in football have the appetite to take on the PFA.

While not all players' agents are, to use Bobby Robson's description of Dennis Roach, 'parasites', it is hard to see what they actually add to the game. Professional football could not survive without players, clubs, governing bodies or fans but the same could not be said of agents. In 2001 English clubs collectively spent £423m on transfer fees; if agents took an average 10 per cent commission, then at least £40m went out of the game. That is a very conservative estimate as it takes no account of commission earned on contract negotiations or endorsements. For a multi-million-pound industry, player agencies are remarkably lightly regulated. The Football Association has the role of regulator in England but, as the Roach case proved, is unable to fulfil that role. FIFA issues the licences but asks no questions as to a person's suitability for the role, beyond that person's ability to pay a deposit. Professionals such as lawyers and accountants are stringently regulated by their own professional bodies, but agents don't even have a body that could regulate themselves. As long as there are high rewards on offer for players, there will be agents, but at least they could be required to put something back into the game, perhaps by paying a proportion of fees earned into the PFA benevolent fund. Agents justify their existence by saying that they ensure that their clients are not unfairly exploited, but the players have a highly effective union that can fulfil that role.

The threatened strike by the PFA in the autumn of 2001 was just the latest in a series of disputes between the union and the rest of football that have occurred since the union's formation. Prior to the threatened strike over the maximum wage and the retain and transfer system in 1960, the threat of strikes had been used to force rises in the maximum wage. With the abolition of this limit the union's role changed somewhat. The successes of 1961 and '63 created a union with a strong membership, a high profile and considerable power in the game. This power was utilised in 1985 when plans for a breakaway Superleague emerged. PFA Chief Executive Gordon Taylor brokered a truce between the warring factions that resulted in a change in the revenue distribution (see Chapter 3) and let it be known that the union would subsequently oppose any changes in the competitive structure that would adversely affect its members. That was enough to kill off the breakaway for a few years as the big clubs had no appetite for a battle with the PFA as well as the small clubs. That the union didn't oppose the formation of the Premier League may seem strange at first, especially as Taylor has spoken of its negative effect on the finances of the game. However, the union's restraint was understandable as its primary purpose was to protect its members' interests, and the increased income on offer would obviously benefit the players. Instead of opposing the formation of the Premier League, Taylor concentrated on securing a proportion of the television revenue that it would generate, an issue that led to the threatened strike of 2001.

The proportion of television money that the PFA received from the League in exchange for the players' televisual performing rights was agreed at 7.5 per cent in 1956, the year after football was first televised. In addition to the 7.5 per cent that was paid to the union, players were paid a fixed fee on a match-by-match basis. The proportion paid to the union was increased to 10 per cent in 1967, and was renewed in 1991, when the flat fee to players was dropped. Although the figure of 10 per cent remained consistent, there is a certain ambiguity as to how it was expressed in the agreement between the union and the League. In 1996 the PFA negotiated deals worth 5 per cent of television income with both the Football League and the Premier League, which was what it demanded when the latest TV deal commenced in 2001.

The Football Association and the Football League decided to hand over negotiations in the dispute to the Premier League, which had the most at stake as it had the largest TV deal. The Premier League's main argument for not paying the 5 per cent was that it was coincidental that the 1996 agreement worked out as 5 per cent and that as no percentage was stated in previous contracts it was not obliged to pay 5 per cent of the new TV deal. Scudamore said at the start of the dispute: 'It is a little bit of a myth, and we need to absolutely nail the fact, that there is no right to 5 per cent or any percentage of our TV money.'[7] The Premier League's initial offer was £30m spread over three years, which compared with the union's demand of £30m per year. Eventually the Premier League offered £50m over three years, with a condition that all but £7m should go to specified PFA welfare funds. The PFA then balloted its membership on strike action with only 22 of the 2,315 who voted, voting against.

Throughout most of the protracted dispute, the Premier League's usually vocal chairmen remained unusually quiet on the issue. Their reticence was a result of their attempt to distance themselves from the dispute. They tried to argue that the PFA's dispute was with the Premier League rather than the clubs. If that was the case they could argue in court that any strike was illegal because the clubs were not actually in dispute with the PFA. Few people outside of the 20 Premier League chairmen accepted this argument as it was understood that the Premier League was merely negotiating on the clubs' behalf and was in fact owned by its member clubs.

From the early days of the dispute to its conclusion, the PFA had the upper hand in the media campaign. There was no shortage of high-profile players who were prepared to defend the PFA's stance, like Arsenal captain Tony Adams:

> The money is not for me but I am the sort of player who might have to strike for everyone to sit up and take notice. It's so youngsters – and 75 per cent of them are out of the game by the age of 21 – can get re-education funding.[8]

Adams and the union highlighted the PFA's benevolent work, not just for younger and retired players, but also the way it assisted clubs who were in financial difficulties. The practice of the PFA loaning financially troubled clubs money to pay players' wages was well established, and in 2001, Hull

City and Chesterfield had been kept afloat by loans from the union. It was this aspect of the union's work that helped to ensure that it had the support of most of the fans. Another reason why the PFA won the media campaign was that most sports journalists were more sympathetic to the union than the Premier League. Support for the Premier League by any journalist could seriously jeopardise his or her future relationship with players. Also Gordon Taylor was a skilled media operator who always returned journalists' calls and stated his case clearly. Put bluntly, he simply delivered better copy than Scudamore or his spokesman Phillip French.

The chairmen broke their vow of silence on the 21 November and Charlton Chief Executive Peter Varney drew attention to the union's comparative wealth: 'The facts are that the union has assets of £17.5m and made a profit of £2m last year. The amount they spent on looking after former and current members was £766,000.' Chelsea Chairman Ken Bates warmed to the theme: 'If the PFA can afford to buy a £2m Lowry painting and invest in Bobby Charlton's soccer schools, why do they need any more money – if indeed, anything at all?' Birmingham City's Chairman David Gold hoped to draw the fans' attention to how lucky players were to be able to earn a living from the game: 'They don't need help from the union when their career finishes. They should just go out and get a proper job.'[9]

With negotiations apparently deadlocked the PFA called a strike for 1 December with the first potential victim a televised match between Chelsea and Manchester United. The Premier League prepared an injunction on the evening of 22 November and the following morning the dispute was settled. The settlement was that the union would receive £52.2m over the three years of the Premier League TV deal, with total discretion as to how it would be spent. After the TV deal expires the union will receive an extra 0.75 per cent for every 1 per cent increase in the value of the deal and if the value of the deal falls, 0.5 per cent less for every 1 per cent. The agreement was for ten years, which justified Taylor's claim: 'We have secured the long-term future of the PFA. In essence it does say that there will be respect for these agreements and there won't be any challenges by anyone to the exact terms and principles of the arrangement.' Future stability was also the key for Scudamore: 'We don't want to go through what we have been through over the last three months at any time in the next three, six or nine years.'[10]

Some within football were disappointed that the Premier League saw the dispute only in terms of money without looking at some of the wider issues of the relationship between the clubs and the PFA. The standard PFA player's contract, which is the basis of all English players' contracts, is highly inflexible. If a player is injured for most of the period of his contract, for example, he is still paid his full rate of pay, and is free to walk away from the club at the end of his contract and join another club. The PFA's insistence that clubs in administration honour all players' contracts in full means that clubs are unable to release players that they can no longer afford to pay. Some flexibility on this issue would actually save the PFA some money as it usually has to loan clubs in administration sufficient funds to honour those contracts. In negotiating a settlement to the 2001 dispute, the Premier League could at least have tried to widen the focus of the talks and wring some concessions out of the PFA over the above and other issues that affect the financial health of the game, but it was only concerned with the bottom line.

It is just as well that the PFA secured significant funding going forward as it will probably need it. As football's financial crisis deepens and clubs face possible closure under the weight of accumulated debt, the PFA will increasingly be called on to assist. Indeed, Bradford City were recent recipients of a £1m loan from the PFA to enable them to pay players' wages while in administration. It is questionable, however, for how long the PFA would be able to assist a Premier League club in administration in a similar fashion.

What was remarkable about the threatened strike of 2001 was the solidarity shown by multi-millionaire Premier League players with their less wealthy colleagues. The average wage in the Third Division was £37,000 per year in 2001, which some Premiership players earned in a week, yet the Premiership players were almost unanimous in their support of the union's stance. Could it be that because players are in many ways still perceived as working-class wage labourers, despite their wealth, they have retained some nineteenth-century working-class values about trade unionism and worker solidarity?

As football's crisis deepens the future for some players looks very uncertain. It could be argued that despite the recent wealth of the English game it simply has too many professional clubs and by implication too many players. Any moves by clubs in the lower leagues to go part-time or semi-professional will be fiercely resisted by the PFA, but it may be the only way they can survive. If there is a substantial decrease in the number of full-time professional clubs, then the PFA will need all of its hard-won resources to retrain players for, as David Gold put it, proper jobs.

## ENDNOTES

[1] Russell, D. 1997. *Football and the English*. London: Carnegie: 22–3.

[2] Inglis, S. 1988. *The Football League and the Men Who Made It*. London: Collins: 220.

[3] www.fifa.com *or* www.thefa.com

[4] www.celticfc.co.uk

[5] www.news.bbc.co.uk/1/hi/sport/football/, 4 June 1999

[6] www.dispatch.co.za/, 7 August 1999

[7] www.news.bbc.co.uk/1/hi/sport/football/, 21 November 2001

[8] *Observer*, 30 September 2001.

[9] www.news.bbc.co.uk/1/hi/sport/football/, 21 November 2001

[10] Ibid.

# 10. Football's Future

CURRENTLY FOOTBALL'S CRISIS IS PUTTING THE IMMEDIATE FUTURE OF AROUND 30 CLUBS IN jeopardy. Bradford City, Bury, Queens Park Rangers, Hull City and Swindon Town are clubs that have gone into administration. Norwich City and Sheffield United have both appealed to their supporters and shareholders for financial support in order to avoid administration. Several other clubs have carried out radical cost cutting, releasing out-of-contract players, and many others plan to do so. Football's financial crisis has led directly to the effective end of Wimbledon as a south London football club. With the exception of Bury, whose plunge into administration was precipitated by the fraudulent activities of its principal benefactor, all the clubs mentioned above have played in the Premier League. Increasing debt levels, uncertainty over future television revenues and spiralling player-wage inflation mean that football's crisis will surely start to affect not only ex-Premier League clubs, but those that are currently members of the Premiership as well.

When Crystal Palace entered administration in 1999, Chairman Mark Goldberg pinned a notice to his office door that read 'administrators are the people who go in after the war is lost and bayonet the wounded', but it is worth noting that no club has been forced out of business and lost to the League since Aldershot in 1992. Queens Park Rangers are just the latest of several clubs that have gone into administration and emerged from it intact. In order for a club to emerge from administration it needs to reach an agreement with creditors and satisfy its football creditors. Football creditors are players who are owed wages and other clubs owed transfer fees, and the Football League's insolvency policy will not allow clubs who have outstanding football debts to compete in the League. In all cases where clubs have come out of administration there has been a cash injection and in some cases loans from the Professional Footballers Association in order to pay players' wages. Cash injections can come from new investors who wish to take over the club, as in the case of Simon Jordan at Crystal Palace, or from supporters, as in the case of Chesterfield where the supporters raised sufficient funds to put the club through a supporters' trust.

That the road to recovery for a club that has been forced into administration usually necessitates a cash injection is hardly surprising, nor is the need for the agreement of creditors to accept a reduced payment for outstanding debts. The problem is that as debt levels rise, the cash injections required increase. Similarly, the agreement of creditors may be harder to secure when the sums they are being asked to write off increase. Therefore, if current trends continue, it is more than possible that a club will go into administration and not be able to emerge from it. In other words, the dynamics of football's crisis will almost certainly lead to a club, or clubs, being liquidated and ceasing to exist. The question is: does that matter?

There is a school of thought that believes if clubs cannot be run as viable businesses then they deserve to fail and go to the wall. It is argued that football clubs are just like any other businesses and they are therefore subject to the commercial reality of the market. As examined in Chapter 2, football clubs share some characteristics with mainstream businesses but are also unique in many other aspects, the most important of these is that their primary purpose is not to make profits. Even the most profitable football club in England, Manchester United, which made £116.4m in pre-tax profits in the five years to 2001, only paid out £23.3m of that profit in dividends, with the bulk of profits reinvested in the development of Old Trafford, the Carrington Academy and buying players. In the 2000–01 season only 18 of the 92 Premier League and Football League clubs made a pre-tax profit and 12 of those were in the Premier League. At the heart of the issue is the question of what football clubs are for. The answer is quite simply that they are to facilitate the playing and watching of football. The model of a limited liability company, as first adopted by Birmingham City in 1888, was adopted so that gate money could be taken and players could be paid wages. It was not the case that companies were set up with the specific purpose of making profits and that they subsequently adopted football clubs as a means to achieve that end. By 1921, 84 clubs had adopted the model of a limited liability company status. Just as the early clubs pre-date the League and formed it for their own ends, so limited liability status was adopted to enable clubs to charge admission and pay wages.

Those who believe that clubs, having embraced the philosophy of the free market, must therefore be subject to the rigours of the market and fold if they are unable to balance their books, also implicitly raises the question of who the clubs are for. The answer to that question is contained in the answer to the question of what they are for. Just as the purpose of clubs is to facilitate the playing and watching of football, so the people for whom they exist are the players and the spectators. It was not, however, the players or the spectators who initiated the move to limited liability company status, it was the club chairmen. The trite response, 'if you live by the market, then so you should die by it', overlooks the fact that players and spectators did not seek to 'live by the market' – it was a decision imposed upon them. Today, of course, many players are more than happy with their position in the market economy, but many spectators or fans, as they are now known, are increasingly questioning theirs.

The most common defence of football clubs against the argument that they should be subject to the same market forces as any other business is their unique role in their local communities. This is a contentious issue as it is fair to say that until relatively recently, clubs often acted as merely another competitor for the local leisure spend. The 1968 Chester Report first suggested the idea that clubs could become more involved in their local communities and in 1978 the Sports Council channelled £1m in grants to clubs for them to set up community schemes but it was a limited success. It was in 1986 that the PFA and the Football League launched the Football in the Community scheme at six clubs in the North West – Manchester City, Manchester United, Preston North End, Oldham Athletic, Bolton Wanderers and Bury – and by the end of the decade over 50 clubs had signed up. The PFA used the scheme as a way of keeping retired players in the game and retraining them as administrators and coaches and there are now over 2,500 people working on schemes throughout the country and over 1,000 ex-players have so far passed through the scheme. Brian Kidd, currently Assistant Manager at Leeds United, became a

Football in the Community officer at Manchester United on retirement from the game and then an assistant to Sir Alex Ferguson before joining Leeds as an assistant to David O'Leary. Activities undertaken involve coaching local children and young offenders, and educational initiatives. It is no coincidence that the scheme was launched at a time when attendances were falling and the game's image was at an all-time low following the events at Heysel and Bradford in 1985 and the rise of hooliganism. If job creation was the objective of the PFA's involvement, then for the Football League it was to increase attendances and repair the game's image. Sceptics point to how little of the funding for Football in the Community schemes actually comes from the clubs themselves and view the exercise as little more than a cynical marketing ploy by some clubs, but the schemes do at least engage the clubs with sections of their local communities beyond those who pay to watch the first team play week in and week out.

In the 2001–02 season an average 1,334,016 people watched English league football on a weekly basis, making it the most popular spectator sport in the country. It also compares favourably with the average Sunday national Church of England attendance of 1,058,000 in October 2000, the last available figure. In many English towns and cities, the football club remains the single largest congregation of the local population and, for this reason alone, it has a social importance beyond the profit and loss and balance sheets of the clubs.

Football's crisis need not be terminal. This book has so far accentuated the negatives in the modern English game but there are still plenty of positives and they hold the key to how the game can not only survive the current crisis, but emerge from it stronger and in a position to avoid further crises. Yes, the game needs wholesale reform but that is surely not beyond the wit of humankind. Part of football's attraction, what makes it the world's number one sport, is its simplicity: 22 players kicking a leather ball with a minimal number of rules. The fundamentals of the football business are also reasonably simple; people play the game and others pay to watch them. To facilitate this simple transaction clubs were formed and eventually they provided stadia so that spectators could be charged an admission fee to watch matches. In order to have some sort of competitive structures and a set of common rules, the FA and the Football League were formed. The FA was essentially a group of players and enthusiasts and the

League was a collective of clubs. After a while, the players formed their own union to represent their interests. Of course the business of football has got a lot more complex over time but it is worth remembering these fundamentals. The simple spectator–player transaction that lies at the heart of the football business has become overshadowed by the very structures that have been created to facilitate it. The interests of the clubs and the governing bodies should really be subservient to the fundamental player–spectator transaction but instead they have come to dominate it. When we look at this transaction in the modern context it becomes abundantly clear that one half of it, the spectators, is grossly under-represented. The spectators provide the money that finances the players, the clubs and the governing bodies, yet they have nobody to represent their interests within the game.

When the author put it to Leeds Chairman Peter Ridsdale that supporters may be unhappy with some of the kick-off times that were demanded by the needs of television, he responded with the proverb 'he who pays the piper calls the tune'. He pointed out that it was TV money that had paid for most of Leeds' expensive squad and that unpopular kick-off times were the price that supporters had to pay and that the attendances at Elland Road were proof that they were willing to do so. Ridsdale would appear to have a point in that in the year to July 2001, £36.62m of Leeds' revenue was generated by television, but only £15.48m was paid by the supporters in gate money. Of course supporters actually fund most of the TV income as well through subscriptions to Sky, but the passive nature of that type of support means that it can have no legitimate voice; if armchair supporters don't like the scheduling of matches, they can cancel their subscriptions. What the worry must be for English football is that if television, for its own reasons, can no longer pay as much as it has, the supporters may have already voted with their feet and deserted the game.

As explained in Chapter 6, television income is a relatively new phenomenon in English football and it is only in the last ten years since the formation of the Premier League and the restructuring and re-branding of the European Cup as the Champions League that television has provided more income than the paying supporter. Even now, according to Deloitte & Touche, the average Premier League club earns around 39 per cent of its income from television and 31 per cent from its paying spectators, with the rest from merchandising, sponsorship and other commercial income. The increase in the proportion of income that comes from television has led to a situation where supporters have become less important to a club financially than broadcasters have. However, as was shown in Chapter 4, when clubs no longer receive high levels of broadcast income, through relegation, it is the supporters who actually fund the club, as traditionally they always have. It should also be noted that when clubs are in dire financial straits, it is the supporters who rally round to save the clubs.

While television is the dominant revenue stream in the Premier League, its importance diminishes in the lower divisions. In 2000, for example, Deloitte & Touche estimated that television would account for 35 per cent of Premier League clubs' income in 2001–02, whereas it would only account for 25 per cent of First Division clubs' revenue. In the Second Division TV would generate 14 per cent and 20 per cent in the Third Division. It would be nice to think that the lower proportion of income earned from television in the lower leagues was due to clubs excelling at maximising other revenue streams, but in reality it merely illustrates how television money is concentrated at the top of the English game.

The lack of television income means that lower league clubs will have to focus on other income streams. Traditionally these have been admission charges, merchandising, sales, catering and corporate-hospitality income. What these have in common is that they are all stadium based. Very few lower league clubs regularly fill their stadia to capacity so there is obviously scope for increasing attendances. This is easier said than done and requires creativity and imagination, particularly in the area of pricing. However, if one of the consequences of football's current crisis is that lower league clubs actively seek to build their brands, increase their supporter bases and fill their stadia, then some good will have come of it. Merchandising in England is generally believed to be flat or in decline at present, but even in a weak merchandising market, retail operations can deliver profits and do not necessarily have to be sited at a stadium, nor do they have to trade exclusively in club merchandise. Stadia are very often underutilised, only being used to stage matches one day every other week during the season. Some clubs, such as Leicester City, have been particularly innovative in using their stadia on non-match days for banqueting and conferencing, both of which can deliver substantial revenue.

Obviously a club's ability to develop stadium-based income streams is contingent on the ownership of the stadium. Where a club does not own its stadium, however, there are still ways in which it can generate non-television revenues. For example, services that are traditionally outsourced, such as catering and publishing, can be brought in house and then marketed to other businesses. Some clubs, such as Leicester and Leeds, have set up subsidiary companies to produce match-day programmes and publications or provide catering services for corporate hospitality, which have become successful operations in their own right, making a significant contribution to the club's bottom line. If the TV bubble does burst, or even just get somewhat deflated, then those clubs that actively sought to develop alternative revenue streams will be the ones who emerge the strongest.

One of the new revenue streams that clubs are looking towards is the Internet. There are parallels between football's current crisis and the dot.com crash of 2000. In fact, some football shares suffered as a result of that crash. Manchester United's share price rocketed in March 2000 following a 'strong buy' recommendation by the brokers Warburg Dillon Read. With the shares having doubled in value in four months, the club was valued on the stock market at £1.1bn and the media was celebrating the world's first billion-pound club. The reasoning behind the surge in the share price was summed up by Warburg analyst Clare Freeman: 'Until recently, nobody was ascribing any value to the club's website. Now, all of a sudden, the website has huge potential to generate revenue and the share price has risen to reflect that.'[1] The reasoning was simple; Internet values were going through the roof and United's website was one of the most visited websites in the UK and other sites with less traffic were seen to be worth a lot of money. At the time the sports website Sportal was in buyout talks with the French TV company Canal Plus with talk of a deal that valued the website operator at £200m plus. By that reckoning, Manchester United's Manutd.com would be worth at least the same so Warburg added £200m to the club's stock market valuation and the shares went through the roof. By the time the Internet boom had turned into bust, Warburg had revised its valuation, valuing Manutd.com at a mere £100m in April 2001. That still justified, in the brokers' eyes, a recommendation that Manchester United shares were a 'strong buy' at 172p, the share price at the time, which valued Man United at £447m. Those in football who claim that the football boom was different from the dot.com boom, and will therefore avoid the same crisis, would do well to remember the £1bn Manchester United headlines and the fact that the club was worth less than half that a year later. Meanwhile Sportal, which failed to conclude a £200m deal with Canal Plus in 2000, was eventually sold in 2002 to ukbetting.com, for £1.

The Internet boom created a thirst for content among dot.com companies. Just as the explosion in the value of football television rights was driven by media companies attempting to establish new platforms – satellite in the early 1990s and digital in the early 2000s – the new media platforms' need for content drove up the value of Internet rights. Premier League clubs, the larger of which had long wanted to market their own television rights themselves rather than give them over to the Premiership to sell collectively, kept their own Internet rights, with the exception of those rights that could be sold to television. So, after the Premier League TV rights from 2001 were sold at the height of the Internet boom in 2000, the only content they could show on their own websites were delayed coverage. Although the technology is not yet up to speed, Premier League clubs can show Saturday matches from midnight on Sunday, while all other games can be viewed on the clubs' websites from midnight the same day they are played. Premier League clubs will be hoping to get more live rights when the current deal expires, and this was the factor behind the setting up of joint venture companies by Arsenal and Liverpool with Granada. The plan is that when enough people have the requisite broadband Internet connection, Liverpool and Arsenal will be able to charge supporters to watch live games through their websites. Currently, however, the appeal of delayed highlights is somewhat limited in the domestic market because supporters can see them for free on terrestrial television.

The Football League was able to cash in at the height of the Internet boom by signing a £65m deal with NTL in June 2000. Under the terms of the deal, NTL subsidiary Premium TV would run all 72 Football League clubs' websites for 20 years. An upfront payment of £25m was paid to the clubs with the remaining £40m paid over the first five years of the deal according to the amount of traffic that each club's site attracted. While each club received a very welcome minimum £300,000, there was some concern over the length of the deal. The reasoning behind the 20-year term was that it would take that amount of time for the Internet to be sufficiently ubiquitous for it to deliver the amount of traffic for the deal to be profitable. However, it does appear that the League has committed itself to an extremely long-term deal which may look very cheap in years to come. This concern was shared by Coventry, who on relegation from the Premier League in 2001 declined the opportunity to join in the deal, preferring instead to retain their Internet rights. Because Premier League clubs have retained their Internet rights, should the Internet eventually deliver the riches that it was once expected to, Premier League clubs will have yet another significant financial advantage over their Football League counterparts.

For Premier League clubs, websites are not as yet delivering significant revenues and their main focus has been to use the Internet to exploit overseas supporters. Manchester United claims to have 50 million supporters worldwide and has been trying to translate that support into money, hence the tour of the Far East in 2001 and the planned tour of the USA in 2003. Other clubs have also tried to exploit the overseas market, with several, Leeds United and Arsenal for example, producing Mandarin-language versions of their websites. However, these efforts have yet to be translated into significant income.

In some ways, the eagerness of the top Premier League clubs to exploit the overseas market is understandable. They are unable to gain many more supporters domestically, and even if they were, most Premier League clubs are regularly filling their stadia so they would not necessarily be able to translate that support into additional income. There is a sense of urgency about the likes of Manchester United, Leeds United, Liverpool, Newcastle United and Arsenal's attempts to conquer potentially lucrative overseas markets. If the next Premier League TV deal is not as valuable as the current one, then the only way that the big clubs will be able to maintain their cost bases, e.g. their player wage bills, and in some cases service their debts, will be to earn additional income from overseas. However, the overseas market is as yet totally unproven and there are several impediments to turning the interest generated by the half a billion people in 130 countries who regularly watch Premier League football into paying customers. In the Far East, for example, there is a thriving market for counterfeit replica kits. Considering that Manchester United's and Arsenal's kit supplier Nike manufactures a lot of its products in the region, it seems somewhat optimistic to expect someone from, say, Thailand to pay a substantial premium for a shirt that was produced locally, just to have the satisfaction of knowing that the majority of that premium is going to the club. Given that most of the Premier League matches that are shown overseas are shown on free-to-air television, it seems unlikely that many people in those countries are going to pay for the privilege of watching games on their computers. The most obvious reason why the Far East may not prove to be the pot of gold that some Premier League clubs expect it to be is the simple fact of the strength of the British pound. Replica shirts may be considered expensive in the UK, but in the Far East they would cost the equivalent of an average worker's weekly wage or more.

While alternative revenue streams may mitigate against a reduction in television income, they will not solve football's crisis if costs are not controlled and the chief cost is of course player wages. The most common answer proposed to the question of spiralling player wages is a system of salary caps as used in American professional sports and recently in Rugby League and Rugby Union in England. There are two types of wage cap, one is where a flat maximum is imposed on all clubs. This would be entirely ineffective in English football because of the massive differences of income even between clubs in the same division. For example the lowest wage bill in the Premier League in 2001–02 was Bradford City's at £16.38m, while the highest was Chelsea's at £52m. Clearly the maximum would have to be set significantly below Bradford's income of £22.89m, which would halve the wage bill of the top five clubs in the wage league table. Those clubs would surely find ways of circumventing such a cap, even if they were persuaded to accept it in the first place. The other form of wage cap is to cap wages as a percentage of turnover. Deloitte & Touche have long advocated a level of turnover of, say, 60 per cent that would be a sustainable level. Like the 'flat cap', such a scheme is hard to police and it doesn't really address the issue of the income gap; 60 per cent of Manchester United's turnover is still more than the total income of the poorest six clubs in the Premier League so setting a wage cap as a percentage of turnover merely maintains the status quo.

The problem with both wage-cap options is that were either to be adopted, then the best players would simply move to play abroad. Therefore any wage cap would have to be Europe wide. There are reasons to believe that wage caps could work at a European level. If UEFA make it a condition that clubs participating in its European competitions adhere to a predetermined wages-to-turnover ratio, the biggest clubs would still have the greatest spending power, but it would be limited. The benefit of wage caps as part of a UEFA licence is that it wouldn't require the support of the FA, Premier or Football Leagues and should be reasonably easy to police, not least because of the limited number of clubs that would need monitoring. The effect of such a scheme would be that the fiscal controls would trickle down throughout the domestic leagues. The player-wage market is very much led by the top clubs. Those clubs that regularly compete in the Champions League use their financial advantage to outbid their domestic rivals for players, thus perpetuating their hegemony. The inflation at the top level then trickles down throughout the league. Control of wages at the top of the English game would have the effect of easing wage inflation throughout the divisions. It would not, however, stop clubs lower down the leagues going for broke in trying to achieve promotion or avoid relegation.

Maximising revenues and controlling costs may sound the logical answer to football's problems as a business, but is only half the story. As has been stated on numerous occasions, and what I hope I have illustrated throughout this book, is that football's financial crisis has been caused by structural issues. It is therefore time to consider those issues and how they can be addressed. There are two structures that dictate the economics of English football: the competitive and the regulatory. That is the structure of the competitions – Leagues and Cups – and the structures of the bodies that regulate the game – the Premier League, the Football League and the Football Association. The regulatory structure has been dealt with extensively so far in this book so it is now time to look at the competitive structure. The two are, however, inextricably linked.

Despite the best intentions of the FA, the Premier League sits at the top of English football's competitive structure. The FA, in its *Blueprint for the Future of Football*, envisaged the national team as sitting on top of football's pyramid, but the success of the Premier League has meant that it, and the FA, has become sublimated to the Premier League clubs. It is not just the political influence of Premier League clubs through the FA board and numerous FA committees that has given the Premier League its dominance. As has been shown, the Premier League also dominates English football on an economic level as clubs attempt to achieve or maintain Premier League status. But such is the Premier League's hegemony that it is now impossible to challenge. Because the voting structure of the Premier League requires a two-thirds majority for any effective change, it is unlikely that any will be forthcoming until such time as two thirds of its clubs have experienced relegation and its devastating financial consequences. Only when two of Arsenal, Manchester United, Liverpool, Chelsea, Aston Villa, Tottenham Hotspur, Southampton or Everton are relegated and their places taken by clubs that have experienced the financial reality of life in the lower divisions, and are prepared to vote for a more equitable sharing of revenues with the other divisions, will the chances of any meaningful change being instigated by the Premier League will improve. Any planned restructuring has therefore got to accept a 20-club (because of the required two-thirds majority the Premier League will never vote to reduce its size) Premier League as a given. Likewise, it has to be accepted that the Premier League will not share any of its revenues with the lower leagues until there is a mass outbreak of philanthropy among its member clubs. It is therefore incumbent on the Football League to restructure itself, something which has been on its agenda since the Premier League was formed in 1992 and the then Crystal Palace Chairman Ron Noades promoted the idea of a Premier League Division Two, which, needless to say, was rejected by the rest of the Premier League.

The purpose of any restructuring of the Football League is to maximise revenues and control costs. The Football League recognised this in 1997, when the pernicious effect of the wealth gap between the Premier and Football Leagues was becoming clearly apparent. The Football League hired Deloitte & Touche as consultants and their recommendations were delivered to the clubs ahead of the 1997 League AGM in June of that year.

Deloitte compared the structure of league football in the four other major European markets (France, Spain, Germany and Italy) and noted that without exception they were organised along regional lines below the top two professional divisions. Deloitte proposed the amalgamation of the Conference into the Third Division, which would be regionalised into a Southern and Northern Division, each comprising 24 clubs. Promotion and relegation between the Second Division and the two regional Divisions would be decided by play-offs and Deloitte suggested that four or five clubs would be promoted or relegated each season.

Regional leagues, it was argued, would increase revenues as they would produce more local derbies. An analysis of attendances at Second and Third Division games found, unsurprisingly, that attendances were generally higher when clubs played other clubs that were geographically closer than when there were considerable distances between them as it was easier for supporters to travel. Of course, local rivalries also play a part. Regionalisation also significantly cuts costs as clubs don't have to pay for their teams to travel or have to pay for overnight accommodation. The additional revenue generated by regionalisation was estimated by Deloitte to be worth between £60,000 and £100,000 a year to each club in gate money. There would be additional revenues generated by the increased attendances in terms of catering sales and possibly enhanced sponsorship income. There were also proposals to revamp the League Cup, to incorporate Conference sides and abolish two-legged ties.

In the event, the clubs rejected Deloitte's recommendations with the then Chester Chairman David Gutterman telling *The Times*:

> The bottom line is that these proposals would mean the Third Division joining the Conference, not the Conference joining the Third Division. As far as I am concerned this was a report that was drawn up just to do the First Division's dirty work.[2]

By that Gutterman meant that the First Division was attempting to re-brand itself by distancing itself from the rest of the League, even though the report advocated keeping the Second Division intact.

While the 1997 Deloitte report was rejected for a number of reasons, not least the Third Division clubs' perception of themselves as fully fledged full-time professional clubs with more in common with their Second Division counterparts as opposed to the semi-professional part-time Conference clubs, perhaps the main reason was that it just did not offer sufficient financial benefits. £100,000 was not considered enough of an incentive for clubs to make such a seismic change when the average annual income of a Third Division club was £1.09m.

Alex Fynn played an important role in the formation of the Premier League, writing many of the proposals contained in the *Blueprint for the Future of Football*, but he maintains that many of the recommendations were overlooked, particularly his advocacy of an 18-club Premier League and for a restructuring of lower-league football. Fynn still maintains that a reorganising of the Football League was imperative for its long-term survival. Unlike Deloitte, Fynn addresses the problems of the First Division as a poor relation of the Premier League and advocates it reducing its size by four clubs to twenty. This, he argues, would reduce the number of dead games as there would be more clubs in contention for play-offs or relegation places. The First Division would then become a showcase for the big clubs who will always find themselves, at times, outside of the Premier League. Fynn also suggests a 20-club Second Division as it would be wrong to relegate relatively large First Division clubs into the relative ignominy of a regional League. Below the Second Division, however, Fynn advocates three regional divisions of 20 clubs with the additional 28 clubs drawn from the Conference and the regional divisions below. Like Deloitte, however, the motivation for Fynn's regionalism is to cut costs incurred by clubs like Carlisle and Torquay when they play each other, while at the same time increasing revenues through the improved interest in local derbies, both to the paying spectator and regional television.

Like the Deloitte proposals, Fynn's regionalism has one fundamental problem: what happens when the clubs relegated from the national Second Division are all drawn from the same region? If three London clubs were relegated from the Second Division to the Southern Regional League, then Fynn says that other clubs would have to change leagues to maintain balance. This, however, would lead to clubs like, say Luton and Northampton, constantly switching from the Southern League to the Midland League, which would not foster the tradition of local rivalries with those clubs. Northampton v. Luton would occur in those seasons when the two happened to be in the same regional division, which itself would be determined by the performance of clubs from different regions rather than the performance of Northampton and Luton. The same would apply to clubs like Stoke City and Mansfield, who would find themselves switching between the Midland and Northern Leagues.

It is not, however, the problems of promotion and relegation that mean that Fynn's proposals are unlikely to be adopted by the League, but once again, the perceived status of the Second and Third Division clubs as semi-professional or part-time. But as Fynn was reported as saying in *The Observer* of 31 March 2002:

> The sacrifice of full-time professional football, in such a grim financial climate, is a small price to pay. This removal of national league status need not be construed as an insult. Going part-time may be a viable option and anyway need not matter as such clubs

would be part of an expanded, strengthened Football League. After all, they can always go full-time if they gain promotion.

Fynn's advocacy of regionalism has a lot to commend it, but just as in 1992 when some of his most important input into the FA's *Blueprint* was ignored, it will probably be the case that his recommendations are ignored because of the self-interest of the clubs as opposed to the good of the game as a whole. That said, if football's financial crisis deepens, a large number of lower-league clubs will have no alternative but to go part-time or semi-professional through simple lack of the finances to do otherwise. Then perhaps they will see the common sense contained in the proposals of Fynn and Deloitte & Touche. As has been noted throughout this book, change in English football always seems to occur in response to crisis, so the scale of the current crisis, 74 out of 92 clubs making losses and combined debts of at least £750m, could lead to the most radical restructuring yet of the Football League. However, this is unlikely to be instigated from below, or with the interests of the whole of football at heart, but from the top in the form of yet another breakaway by the larger First Division clubs.

The collapse of the £315m three-year ITV Digital deal and its eventual replacement with the £95m four-year Sky deal has left First Division clubs with a considerable shortfall, estimated to be around £2m per year. The revenue distribution mechanisms of the Football League mean that around 40 per cent of the total paid by Sky will go to the Second and Third Divisions, even though those two divisions will provide only 10 of the 66 games that Sky will show each season. Faced with a potentially disastrous shortfall, the First Division, or more likely its 20 largest clubs, may well decide to breakaway from the rest of the Football League and renegotiate a deal of similar value with Sky, but keep 100 per cent of the proceeds. There would be no objection from the Premier League and the FA would rightly be accused of hypocrisy if it blocked such a breakaway after its sanctioning of the 1992 Premier League breakaway. At the time of writing it is unlikely that such a breakaway could occur before the start of the 2002–03 season, although there are already murmurings about it from some First Division chairmen. But as football's crisis deepens, the likelihood of it taking place in time for the start of the 2003–04 season will increase.

Football's crisis is not only economic but also political. It is political in the sense that the governance of the game is carried out by a relatively small elite that has its own interests, and not those of the game as a whole, as its primary motivation. The board of the Football Association may be slightly biased in favour of the amateur game, but the professional game holds the purse strings. There are five places on the twelve-man – and of course it is all men – board for the professional game and four of those are occupied by Premier League chairmen. The 92 FA council members who are meant to be the ultimate authority in the English game represent a wide range of interests – the universities, the armed forces and even the women's game – but there are two groups who are conspicuous by their absence: the players and the supporters. Given their importance to the game, which is fundamental, this seems anomalous to say the least. While the players have the PFA to represent their interests, the supporters have had no one to represent theirs. But that could be about to change with the increase of supporter activism and the rise of the supporters' trust movement.

The activism of football supporters is a relatively modern phenomenon and it is surely no coincidence that it has occurred as the supporters' financial influence on the game has diminished. The pioneers of supporter activism were undoubtedly the supporters of Charlton Athletic whose triumphant campaign to return the club to the Valley is detailed in Chapter 4 and served as an inspiration to the supporters' trust movement by showing how a well-organised group of supporters could achieve the seemingly impossible. The rise of the supporters' trust movement has largely been in response to the clubs plunging into financial crisis. The earliest example of a supporters' trust was at Northampton Town in 1992. When the club was plunged into administration with £1.6m of debt, the supporters raised £90,000. This was used to purchase 7 per cent of the share capital of the post-administration club and to secure a place on the board. The motivation was to ensure that the club was run on a sound financial footing and that further crises could be averted. Since then trusts have been formed at 45 English clubs, 22 have bought shareholdings in their clubs and 16 have members on the boards of clubs. At Swindon Town, Lincoln City, Bournemouth and Brighton and Hove Albion the trusts have proved crucial in ensuring the clubs' survival, while at Chesterfield the supporters actually own the club, having raised £10,000 to buy it out of administration. Supporters' trusts are not confined to lower-league clubs: Aston Villa, Newcastle and Tottenham Hotspur supporters have formed trusts and even Manchester United have a trust that regularly meets with the board. The United trust, Shareholders United, was formed by shareholder supporters who had successfully campaigned against Sky's 1999 attempted takeover of United, which surely represents the greatest success of any supporter group to date. If one of the world's largest media companies can have its plans to take over the 'richest club in the world' thwarted by a group of well-organised supporters, then supporters everywhere can be reassured that their influence can be harnessed and made effective. More recently, the achievements of the Wimbledon Supporters' Trust in establishing AFC Wimbledon in response to their club's relocation to Milton Keynes has been quite remarkable. To set up a club with a team of players, a coach, a stadium to play in (in south-east London of course), a six-figure sponsorship deal and gain admission to the Southern Counties League in around six weeks, and without a wealthy benefactor in sight, shows yet again how much can be achieved when supporters organise themselves around a common aim. As more and more clubs are realising that their relationship with their supporters does not have to be solely exploitive and are inviting supporters' representatives on to their boards, perhaps it won't be too long before there is an FA Council seat, or better still, a place on the FA board for someone who genuinely has the interests of supporters at heart. Perhaps, for example, the chairman of Supporters Direct, or someone elected by a national ballot of supporters' trust members nationwide.

Football's crisis is deep and wide-ranging, but it need not be terminal. There are enough forward-looking people within the game who are prepared to look beyond their narrow self-interest to make a difference as to how the game responds to the crisis. In this book I have tried not to personalise the issues that have contributed to the current crisis, but it is fair to say that some names appear more often than others. I have tried to show that the problems afflicting the modern game are structural rather than the result of the actions of certain individuals but such is the concentration of the power in the hands of relatively few people, that the structural changes required for the game to survive will have to be instigated by those individuals, or more likely their immediate successors. Such is the scale of football's crisis that reform needs to be wide ranging and thorough, and it needs to happen now. A change in personnel at the top of the game will not in itself lead the game out of crisis, but it would be a start. More important than a change of personnel is a change in the mind set of those running the game. Recognition of the fact that the game is in crisis and an understanding of why this is, would be the first step towards the game emerging from it. I hope that this book in some small way contributes to that understanding.

## ENDNOTES

1   www.CFOEuropean.com, April 2000.
2   *Soccer Analysis* (3), May 1997: 7.

# Bibliography and Sources

## FINANCIAL SOURCES

The financial figures quoted are primarily these two sources: club reports and accounts, and the *Deloitte & Touche Survey of Football Club Accounts 1993 to 1995* and the *Annual Reviews of Football Finance 1996 to 2002*. Wherever possible, figures pertaining to individual clubs are sourced from the club's accounts, while the sectorial information, e.g. turnover, debt and player wages by division and league, has been gleaned from the *Deloitte & Touche* reports. Some references to player wages for clubs not listed on the stock exchange have also come from the *Deloitte & Touche* reports. Statements from clubs to the stock exchange have been sourced from the stock exchange Regulatory News Service, which can be accessed via the Internet at http://www.hemscott.com/equities.

## BOOKS

Butler, B. 1987. *The Football League 1888–1988* London: Queen Anne Press

Conn, D. 1997. *The Football Business*. Edinburgh: Mainstream

Deloitte & Touche. Annual. *Annual Review of Football Finance*

Dempsey, A. and Reilly K. 1998. *Big Money, Beautiful Game*. London: Nicholas Brealey

Fynn, A. and Guest, L. 1994. *Out of Time*. London: Simon & Schuster

Hamil, S., Michie, J., Oughton, C. and Warby, S. 2001. *The Changing Face of the Football Business*. London: Frank Cass

Hamil, S., Michie, J., Oughton, C. and Warby, S. 2000. *Football in the Digital Age*. Edinburgh: Mainstream

Inglis, S. 1988. *The Football League and the Men Who Made It*. London: Collins

King, A. 2002. *End of the Terraces*. London: Continuum

Russell, D. 1997. *Football and the English*. London: Carnegie

Tomas, J. 1971. *The Leeds United Story*. London: Arthur Barker

Sugden, J. and Tomlinson, A. 1998. *FIFA and the Contest for World Football*. Cambridge: Polity Press

Szymanski, S. and Kuypers, T. 1999. *Winners and Losers: The Business Strategy of Football*. London: Penguin

## REPORTS

The Football League. 1990. *One Game, One Team, One Voice.*

The Football Association. 2002. *Decision on the matter of Wimbledon FC and the proposed move to Milton Keynes.*

The Football Association. 1991. *A Blueprint for the Future of Football.*

House of Commons Culture Media and Sport Committee. 2001. Staging International Sporting Events Third Report Volume II. London: HMSO

Monopolies and Mergers Commission. 1999. *British Sky Broadcasting Group plc and Manchester United plc: Report on the proposed merger.*

Restrictive Practices Court. 1999. *Judgement on the case brought by the Office of Fair Trading against the Football Association Premier League and British Sky Broadcasting.*

## MAGAZINES AND JOURNALS

*Business Age, Football Business International, Singer & Friedlander Football Review, Sport Business, Stadia Business, Soccer Analyst, Soccer Investor, World Soccer*

## NEWSPAPERS

*The Guardian, Daily Telegraph, Financial Times, The Independent, London Evening Standard, Mail on Sunday, News of the World, The Observer, Sunday Telegraph, Sunday Times, The Times*

## WEBSITES
### For general football news:

www.ananova.com

www.bbc.co.uk/sport

**For club records, attendances, transfers and results:**
Attendances: www.european-football-statistics.co.uk
Football Club History Database: www.fchd.btinternet.co.uk
Transfers: www.footballtransfers.co.uk
General: www.soccerbase.com
International: www.rsssf.com

**For the business of football:**
The Political Economy of Football:
     www.members.tripod.com/~WynGrant/WGFootballPage
www.Sportbusiness.com
www.Soccerinvestor.com

**Supporter sites:**
Nottingham Forest: www.the-eye.com
Bradford City: www.boyfrombrazil.co.uk
Supporters' Trusts: www.supporters-direct.org
Clubs in Crisis: www.clubsincrisis.com
Wimbledon: www.wisa.org.uk

# Index